T0331414

"A very clear, readable and concise introduction to accounting which would suit both students of the subject and also non-specialists who want to get a quick grasp of the territory."

David Wornham, Principal Lecturer,
University of the West of England, UK

"This book explains concepts of management accounting and financial management, from the first principles, with a clear approach and with strong emphasis on the applications to financial managers, yet without lacking in academic rigour and depth. It is particularly suitable for those with limited financial and accounting expertise that through very well designed activities and examples will achieve an impressive level of knowledge and analysis in the subject."

Vasco Vendrame, Senior Lecturer,
University of the West of England, UK

"A very welcome, concise and easy to read contribution to accounting literature that makes core accounting concepts understandable in a straightforward way."

Michael Davies, Senior Lecturer,
University of West of England, UK

Management Accounting for Beginners

Accounting skills are increasingly important in many walks of life. In education, these skills are becoming vital beyond business, accounting and economics students; in work, accounting is no longer an outsourced specialism across all sectors. This concise book provides readers with a primer on accounting which focuses on its uses for managers.

Beginning with the basics of financial accounting, the main part of the book focuses on the more applicable role and use of management accounting. Topics covered include budgeting, break-even analysis, performance measurement and investment appraisal. Features to aid understanding include worked activities, discussion points and numerical examples with answers.

This unique and focused text will be welcomed by all those looking to develop an employable competency in accounting and finance.

Nicholas Apostolides graduated from Lancaster University in 1972 with a degree in Economics, and completed the MBA in Finance at City University in 1984. In between he has worked in retail management, tourism, accountancy and as an economist. He is a senior lecturer at Bristol Business School, and was the programme director for the CM/DMS and deputy director for the MBA. He has represented the University at British Council Fairs in Athens, Hong Kong and Nicosia, and is also a member of the Chartered Management Institute. He completed his PhD on the subject of company annual general meetings in 2012.

Management Accounting for Beginners

Nicholas Apostolides

Routledge
Taylor & Francis Group
LONDON AND NEW YORK

First published 2016
by Routledge
2 Park Square, Milton Park, Abingdon, Oxon OX14 4RN

And by Routledge
711 Third Avenue, New York, NY 10017

First issued in paperback 2017

*Routledge is an imprint of the Taylor & Francis Group,
an informa business*

British Library Cataloguing in Publication Data
A catalogue record for this book is available from the British
Library

Library of Congress Cataloging-in-Publication Data
Names: Apostolides, Nicholas, author.
Title: Management accounting for beginners / Nicholas Apostolides.
Description: Abingdon, Oxon ; New York, NY : Routledge, 2016. |
    Includes bibliographical references and index.
Identifiers: LCCN 2015037252 | ISBN 9781138641570 (hardback) |
    ISBN 9781315630410 (ebook)
Subjects: LCSH: Managerial accounting.
Classification: LCC HF5657.4 .A66 2016 | DDC 658.15/11—dc 3
LC record available at http://lccn.loc.gov/2015037252

ISBN 13: 978-0-8153-5122-1 (pbk)
ISBN 13: 978-1-138-64157-0 (hbk)

Typeset in Times
by Apex CoVantage, LLC

Contents

Glossary

Absorption costing (or full costing)   an accounting method that calculates the costs of a product or service by adding together all the costs – fixed as well as variable – and dividing by the number produced.

Accounts payable (also referred to as creditors)   amounts owing to trade suppliers and other sundry creditors, usually payable within one year.

Accounts receivable   (also referred to as debtors) amounts owed by customers.

Activity-based costing (ABC)   a costing approach originally devised by Kaplan and Cooper in the 1980s which is intended to bring about a better understanding of overheads and to create a more efficient form of cost control. Costs are assigned to the activities that are the cause of the overhead (known as cost pools) and then charged to the products that are actually demanding those activities (referred to as cost drivers).

Allocation   the portion of a company's overheads which can be charged directly to a cost centre.

Amortisation   similar to depreciation and usually applied to intangible non-current assets such as leases or **goodwill**, writing off a non-current asset over time.

Apportionment   the process whereby costs are spread over various cost centres, for example according to floor area or head count.

Appropriation account   the part of the income statement showing how ownership funds are dispersed.

Balance sheet (now called the statement of financial position)   records the assets and liabilities on a particular day.

Balanced scorecard   a strategy tool for measuring performance, first devised by Kaplan and Norton, comprising financial, customer, internal and learning perspectives.

Break-even point   the activity level at which the organisation is making neither profit nor loss, i.e. total revenues equal total costs.

Budget   a financial plan prepared prior to a defined period of time for the purpose of meeting specific objectives.

Capital expenditure   purchase of non-current assets such as buildings, machines or vehicles for business use.

Consolidated accounts (also known as **group accounts**)   the final accounts of all the companies in a group of which 51% or more of the shares are owned, joined together and treated as if it were a single company.

Contribution   a measure of profit based on the difference between sales revenue and variable costs.

Conventional budgeting (also known as incremental budgeting)   using previous years' budgets as the basis for the current year, subject to adjustments.

Cost centre   a location, function or group of activities for which costs can be attributed.

Cost of capital   the interest rate relating to the cost of funds used to finance a project.

Cost driver   the factor causing a change in an activity's cost.

Cost pool   a collection of costs associated with a particular business activity or cost driver.

Creditors (also known as accounts payable)   amounts owing to trade suppliers and other sundry creditors, usually payable within one year.

Current assets   the short-term assets used for running an enterprise, comprising inventories, accounts receivable and cash.

Current liabilities   debts payable within a year, such as accounts payable, bank overdraft, proposed dividend and taxation.

Debentures   a form of loan stock issued by companies at a fixed rate of interest and repayable on a specified date.

Debtors (also referred to as accounts receivable)   amounts owed by customers.

Depreciation   the decrease in value of a non-current asset over time through wear and tear.

Direct labour   the labour costs, usually in the form of wages, associated with shop-floor staff involved with the conversion process of a product or service.

Direct materials   raw materials which can be assigned to the production of a good or service.

Discounted cash flow   a technique for translating future cash flows into their present value equivalent using a specified rate of interest.

Dividend   the proportion of profits a company distributes to shareholders, expressed in terms of pence per share.

Equity the net worth or shareholders' interest in a company, showing the value of share capital and reserves attributable to owners.

Exception reporting a system that documents what is abnormal and therefore focuses attention for correction.

Final accounts (also referred to as financial statements) the income statement, **statement of cash flows** and statement of financial position.

Financial accounting the preparation of financial statements to external users of information, primarily shareholders.

Financial ratio the relationship between two or more financial values, expressed as a percentage, fraction or ratio.

Financial statements (also referred to as final accounts) the income statement, statement of cash flows and statement of financial position.

Fixed assets (now called non-current assets) the assets a business needs to carry out trade such as buildings, machines and vehicles.

Fixed costs costs which are unaffected by the level of activity, such as rent.

Gearing refers to the balance sheet funding provided by sources other than the owners.

Goodwill classed as an **intangible asset**, it shows the difference between the amount paid for an enterprise and the net value of the assets acquired.

Group accounts (also known as **consolidated accounts**) the final accounts of all the companies in a group of which 51% or more of the shares are owned, joined together and treated as if it were a single company.

Incremental budgeting (also known as conventional budgeting) using previous years' budgets as the basis for the current year, subject to adjustments.

Indirect costs (or overheads) costs not directly related to the production of a good or a service, such as administrative salaries or straight-line depreciation.

Intangible assets assets which have value but are not physical in nature, such as intellectual property, patent rights, brands and goodwill.

Internal rate of return (IRR) a project appraisal technique showing the rate of return achieved when the sum of the discounted cash flows is equal to the original capital outlay, i.e. the net present value is zero.

Inventories (also known as stock or stock-in-trade) raw materials, **work-in-progress** and finished goods, usually shown at the lower of cost or market value.

Investment appraisal (also known as project appraisal or capital budgeting) is a collection of techniques, such as payback, NPV or IRR, used to identify the attractiveness of an *investment*.

Just-in-time an inventory control system, receiving goods and components only when they are needed in the production process to save on waste and to maximise efficiency.

Key performance indicator (KPI) a measurable value that demonstrates how effectively a company is achieving key business objectives.

Long-term liabilities (now known as non-current liabilities) debt which is not due for repayment for a year or more.

Management accounting financial information intended mainly for the benefit of managers.

Marginal costing an accounting method that calculates the costs of a product or service by considering only the variable costs.

Master budget the overall summary of an organisation's plans, comprising forecast income statement, cash flows and financial position.

Net current assets (also known as working capital) current assets minus current liabilities.

Net present value (NPV) a highly regarded investment appraisal technique which uses discounted cash flow to show the sum of the present values of incoming and outgoing cash flows over time.

Non-current assets (formerly called fixed assets) the assets a business needs to carry out trade, such as buildings, machines and vehicles.

Non-current liabilities (formerly known as long-term liabilities) debt which is not due for repayment for a year or more.

Overheads (or indirect costs) costs not directly related to the production of a good or a service, such as administrative salaries or straight-line depreciation.

Payback the time taken for the cash flows of a capital project to equal the original outlay, normally expressed in years.

Prime costs the direct costs of a commodity in terms of materials and labour.

Profit revenue minus costs.

Profit centre a business unit or department within an organisation that generates revenues and profits or losses.

Purchases items bought for the purpose of re-sale.

Residual value sometimes called scrap value, the amount expected to be obtained from the disposal of a non-current asset at the end of its useful life.

Responsibility accounting the reporting and analysis of financial information about decision centres within an organisation.

Sales Income derived from the principal activity of an organisation by exchanging goods or services for money, usually shown net of VAT.

Standard cost the estimated cost of performing an operation or producing a good under normal conditions.

Statement of cash flows shows incomings and outgoings of cash, broken down into operating, investing and financing activities.

Statement of financial position (formerly called the balance sheet) records the assets and liabilities on a particular day.

Straight-line depreciation a method of depreciation calculated by deducting the residual value of a non-current asset from its cost and dividing the result by the number of years it is expected to be used.

Trial balance a book-keeping report listing all the debit and credit balances, with an error being indicated if the two totals do not match.

Variable costs costs which increase as the level of activity goes up, such as direct materials.

Variance analysis a key element of performance management whereby the difference between budgeted and actual costs is calculated and explained.

Work-in-progress the value of partly completed manufactured goods.

Working capital (also known as net current assets) current assets minus current liabilities.

Zero-based budgeting a method of budgeting where every item must be justified and approved, without reference to the past.

1 Why are you doing this?

For success in any career you need to be able to control those activities you are responsible for by making good use of what you encounter daily and by sorting data in order to provide meaningful information. This requirement is especially significant in the field of business, for if you can't make sense of a bottom-line figure, you could be in trouble. Whether you are reading this book as a:

- student
- employee
- owner
- manager
- public-sector worker
- private-sector worker
- voluntary-sector worker
- profit-seeking businessperson
- charity administrator
- large organisations
- small organisations
- manufacturing industry professional
- service industry professional

a basic knowledge of finance and accounting will stand you in good stead for the rest of your life. The principal objective of this book is to improve your understanding of the financial aspects of business in order to improve your effectiveness, whether as a student or as a manager. It may not turn you into a fount of all knowledge, but it can make you wiser and more satisfied in your role. Sometimes wisdom can involve asking the right questions rather than being able to supply the right answers. To do this you need to ensure that your numeracy skills – however weak at the outset – can be developed and sharpened so that you can carry out a wide range of functions confidently and knowledgeably. The results could transform your life, giving you a platform for academic success and career enhancement.

Types of accounting

Accounting is the way financial information is prepared, disclosed and conveyed. It is used by commercial businesses as well as by non-profit-seeking organisations alike for the interest and edification of a variety of users including:

- suppliers
- banks
- investors
- creditors
- competitors
- managers
- government
- regulators
- customers
- lobby groups
- local communities
- interested observers.

Accounting can be divided into two main categories, financial accounting and management accounting. **Financial accounting** deals mainly with the preparation of **financial statements** for external users of information, primarily shareholders and other types of investors. These statements are required by law for the past financial year and tend to be backward looking, covering every area of the organisation. The resulting report and accounts are usually audited by accounting firms, themselves staffed by qualified financial accountants. Chapters 2 and 3 deal primarily with financial accounting.

Management accounting is the main focus of the rest of this book. It is more likely to be practiced by internal users of financial information mainly for the benefit of managers, many of whom may not be specialists in finance but come from backgrounds such as business administration, marketing or human resources. Management accounting reports tend to be forward looking and can be generated daily, weekly, monthly or yearly to facilitate future cost control, income generation and managerial decision making.

Management accounting for beginners

This book is intended for a wide range of potential readers, from first-time students of finance and accounting to practising managers who may have substantial experience but no formal qualifications in the subject. It aims to provide non-accounting specialists with the essential tools for seeing the overall picture when faced with a complex maze of jargon and figures, letting you understand them in a concise manner, taking a minimum of time and effort. The many skills dealt with here include how to assess and interpret financial performance, the effective management of working capital, cost awareness and the ability to monitor budgets as well as an understanding of project appraisal techniques. Clear guidance and illustrative examples will be provided to help students and managers control resources and justify proposals for expenditure by setting objectives, recognising alternative options, utilising the appropriate financial techniques and taking into account some of the non-financial aspects of managerial decision making. In the end many of the mysteries and technicalities of accounting will be made clear in a way that enables the application and implementation of practical methods successfully for the future. The generality of focus is deliberate, as it is intended to cover the basics in a very fundamental and uncomplicated manner to allow even complete novices a degree of insight and understanding of concepts and techniques which will become indispensable to their futures.

Topics covered:

- *Double-Entry Book-Keeping* – This section provides an introduction to keeping formal accounting records by means of debit and credit entries.
- *Interpreting Financial Statements* – The key financial statements showing profitability, cash flow and the balance sheet position are prepared and explained.
- *Budgeting* – This chapter examines the contribution that forecasting future business activity makes to business efficiency.
- *Cost Behaviour and Classification* – Fixed and variable costs and the principles of cost identification are presented and explained.
- *Break-Even Analysis* – The break-even concept is explained and calculated, showing how much business activity needs to be achieved before profits are forthcoming.
- *Marginal and **Absorption Costing*** – This technique compares differing cost approaches and the financial as well as non-financial-factors ways to assess results.
- *Overhead Recovery* – When pricing products and services, it is not only the obvious material and labour costs which must be borne in mind; methods of accurately assessing the hidden overhead costs are vital, too.
- *Activity-Based Costing* – The use of **activity-based costing** (ABC) is explained as an alternative basis for tracking and controlling overheads.

- *Performance Measurement* – The **balanced scorecard** provides a useful starting point for assessing the performance of a business and its members.

- *Variance Analysis* – The difference between budgeted figures and actual results provides a powerful basis for assessing and controlling business performance.

- *Responsibility Accounting* – Tracing costs and revenues to the people or departments that have incurred them is examined here.

- *Investment Appraisal* – The financial merits of whether to go ahead with a project, whether large or small, are demonstrated here.

Each chapter has a worked Activity to illustrate the concept being dealt with. There are also general Discussion Points to give you a chance to think about the concepts involved, exchange views on their significance and apply them to a chosen organisation. This could be your school or employer or else, for those with limited work experience, it can be somewhere you are familiar with, perhaps by shopping there or having someone you know working there. Each chapter also has a representative numerical Example, with answers provided at the end of the book.

Information technology

It is worth mentioning that the knowledge and skills involved in mastering – or at least developing a useful proficiency in – word processing, spreadsheets, Internet research and other software applications are becoming increasingly important and expected as second nature in all walks of life. In business, information is king. Computer technology enables you to be innovative and productive, and today's business world requires competence in this area along with the ability to use built-in software tools such as graphics, spellcheckers, dictionaries, thesauruses and many other technological applications to help you collect, process and present information clearly and precisely. It gives you the opportunity to lead by example, control your own output and raise the quality of your own work. More than anything, though, information technology offers a creative and flexible tool to enhance your effectiveness and improve your working environment. Ally this to a basic understanding of how financial information is prepared and communicated, and your business potential will be assured.

2 Double-entry book-keeping

Chapter overview

The accurate and timely recording of financial information is vital for any type of business. Apart from enabling those who need this information to access it (such as tax authorities, banks or potential buyers), tidy records allow managers to keep track of how much they owe (called **creditors** or **accounts payable**) and are owed (termed **debtors** or **accounts receivable**). In addition, well-kept accounts allow managers to keep a regular eye on the cash requirements of the business, its profitability and how much it is worth.

In this chapter we will take a broad look at the language of book-keeping and examine the applications and content of the principal forms of corporate financial statements to allow managers to know everything that's happened up to a particular date.

The nature of double entry

The universal language for recording business transactions is double-entry book-keeping, with a tradition dating back to even before the Franciscan friar Luca Pacioli and the Italian merchants of the fifteenth century. It is based on the principle of listing every figure twice – once on the left (debit) and once on the right (credit). It is worth pointing out that there is no great value in ascribing 'good' or 'bad' to these words as we do when we use the words 'debit' and 'credit' in everyday language. It is much better in this context to regard them simply as meaning, respectively, 'left' and 'right'.

The general layout for double entry follows basic rules. When entering cash or bank entries, *money received* goes on the debit side (abbreviated to Dr) and *money paid out* goes on the credit side (abbreviated as Cr). Asset accounts, such as machines or purchases of goods, are shown on the left, and liabilities, such as creditors or bank loans, appear on the right. Expense accounts (e.g. rent, wages) have a debit balance, while revenue accounts (such as **sales**) are on the credit side.

This chart summarises the main points:

Table 2.1 Double-entry chart

DEBIT (Dr)	CREDIT (Cr)
Cash in	Cash out
Assets	Liabilities
Expenses	Revenues

Transactions are normally organized into four main books or ledgers, although nowadays this is more likely to occur electronically on a computer software package which takes care of such details automatically.

The four books are:

- The *Cash Book*, usually with separate columns for cash and bank entries.
- The *Sales Ledger* for credit customers (debtors or accounts receivable).
- The *Purchases Ledger*, sometimes called the Bought Ledger, for credit suppliers (creditors or accounts payable).
- The *Nominal Ledger*, sometimes called the General Ledger or Journal, which contains all the other accounts not dealt with in the other three books (expenses, revenues, assets, liabilities, sales, purchases and so on).

For the purpose of notation of double-entry transactions *T-accounts* are used as a visual aid, with debits to the left of the vertical bar and credits to the right.

A simple case will allow us to look at how a day's transactions can be recorded using double entry:

Activity: It is Barton Hill's first day of trading. He borrows £20,000 from the bank and buys a van for £8,000 cash goods for resale on credit for £2,000. He pays rent of £500 and fills the petrol tank for £50 (both with cash). A customer buys some of the goods on credit for £700.

According to the chart in Table 2.1, the first transaction, borrowing from the bank, will appear as £20,000 on the debit, or left, side of Barton's Cash Book (as it is cash in) and £20,000 on the credit, or right, side of the Loan Account in the Nominal Ledger (as the bank loan is a liability, i.e. a debt which Barton is due to repay eventually).

Buying the van means that £8,000 goes on the debit side of the Van Account in the Nominal Ledger (asset) and £8,000 on the credit side of the Cash Account (money out).

Buying goods for resale, termed purchases: £2,000 goes on the left of the Purchases Account in the Nominal Ledger (goods are an asset). As the transaction was on credit, £2,000 also goes on the right side of the supplier's named account in the Purchases Ledger (the fact that the supplier is now Barton's creditor- i.e. someone to whom Barton owes money – means that they are shown on the credit side, as a liability).

The rent of £500 appears on the left of the Rent Account in the Nominal Ledger (expense) and to the right of the Cash Account (cash out).

Petrol is an expense, so it shows on the left of the Petrol Account in the Nominal Ledger and on the right of the Cash Account (cash out).

Finally, the £700 sale goes to the right of the Sales Account in the Nominal Ledger (revenue) and, since the customer is now a debtor, £700 goes on the left of the named debtor account in the Sales Ledger (Barton's debtors owe money to him, so they are classed as an asset).

So the Double-Entry Chart shows how transactions appear either on the debit or credit side of the individual T-accounts within the various ledgers.

The trial balance

At the end of the period – in this case a single day – Barton can add up all his debits and credits to see if everything balances and as a preparation for preparing his main financial statements. By *balancing off* any account with multiple entries – in this example, only the Cash Account needs balancing off – he can see his final figures at the end of the day. The Cash Account has entries of £20,000 cash in on the debit side (cash in) and purchases of £8,000, rent of £500 and petrol of £50 on the credit side (cash out). The balancing figure is therefore £11,450, which is carried down (c/d) on the credit side to make both sides balance and brought down (b/d) on the left to show how much is left in the cash account for the next period.

Table 2.2 Cash account

Date	Bank Loan	20,000	date	Purchases	8,000
			date	Rent	500
			date	Petrol	50
			date	Balance c/d	11,450
		20,000			20,000
	Balance b/d	11,450			

If we now list all the amounts shown in each of the accounts we can see the **trial balance** for the business as at the end of trading on Barton's first day.

Table 2.3 Trial balance as at (date)

	Dr £	Cr £
Cash	11,450	
Bank Loan		20,000
Van	8,000	
Purchases	2,000	
Rent	500	
Petrol	50	
Sales		700
Debtor	700	
Creditor		2,000
	22,700	22,700

Types of trial balance errors

If both sides do not balance it means that double entry has not been carried out properly, and we must look through everything to find the mistake. Even if they do eventually balance it is certainly a good sign but not a guarantee that all is well. Mistakes may still have been made, for example:

- An *error of omission* where a figure has been completely left out.
- An *error of commission* where entries have been made into the wrong account.
- An *error of original entry* where the wrong figure has been used.
- An *error of reversal* where the debit figure has been put on the right instead of the left and vice versa.
- *Compensating errors* occur, perhaps by chance, when unrelated errors cancel each other out.

The role of book-keeping

Knowing how to keep double-entry records is largely a clerical function, and many supervisors and managers may not feel the need to know the intricate details unless they are specifically involved in the activity of keeping the books. This is probably even more likely to be the case where software packages (or paid accountants) can take care of the practicalities instead.

However, it is important to understand how the double-entry accounting records and trial balance eventually lead to the **final accounts** of a business. The resulting profitability statement, cash flow and balance sheet are important documents, and they give valuable clues as to the health of the organisation for all the people involved in viewing them, whether they are managers, supervisors, employees, customers, suppliers or investors. This is the subject of our next chapter.

Summary

This chapter has covered:

- The concept of double-entry and the principles of book-keeping.
- T-accounts and the concept of the trial balance.
- Types of trial balance errors.

Discussion Point 1: What different types of sensitive information are held within organisations?

Discussion Point 2: Provide reasons it is better for a businessperson to record and retain financial information rather than relying on word of mouth or memory.

Discussion Point 3: How can you ensure that people keeping sensitive information always follow correct procedures for storage and disclosure?

Exercise: Carry out the double entries for the following transactions and produce a trial balance as at December 31 for Clarence Park's business:

Jan 10	Purchase of a vehicle for £5,000 (cheque).
Jan 23	Purchase of a machine for £3,000 (cheque).
Feb 7	Purchase of goods for £2,000 from Gurney Slade on credit.
Feb 8	Clarence returns £100 worth to Gurney as faulty.
Mar 9	£1,000 worth of goods sold for cash.
Mar 10	Clarence borrows cash £6,000 from the bank.
Apr 2	£500 goods sold to Kingston Seymour on credit.
Apr 10	Kingston returns £200 worth as damaged.
Apr 16	£400 sold to Heath End on credit.
May 26	Clarence buys £200 worth of goods from Gurney Slade for cash and £300 on credit.
May 31	Clarence sends off a cheque for £200 for rent.
Jun 4	Clarence withdraws £200 from the bank and goods worth £100 from the business (for private use).

Jun 10	He buys £500 of goods on credit from Stanton Drew.
Jul 12	Kingston Seymour pays £100 of his debt to Clarence by cheque and receives a discount of £10 (£110 in all).
Jul 30	Cash sales £2,000.
Aug 4	Purchase of goods for £600 from Stanton Drew on credit, including £100 carriage in.
Aug 18	Clarence pays his staff £1,000 wages.
Sep 10	Kingston Seymour defaults and is unable to pay his debts.
Sep 16	Clarence pays £300 cash to Stanton Drew and receives a further £100 discount (£400 in all).
Oct 15	£600 sold to Clay Hill on credit.
Oct 31	Clarence pays sundry expenses of £100 in cash.
Nov 5	Clay Hill pays £550 cash and receives £50 discount (£600 total).
Nov 21	Heath End pays £100 by cheque.
Nov 24	Heath's cheque bounces.
Dec 21	Clarence repays the bank £1,000 of the loan, plus interest of £400.
Dec 26	He sells the machine for £2,900 cash.

3 Interpreting financial statements

Chapter overview

Accounting skills are increasingly important for a successful career in any field, and the ability to interpret financial statements is the perfect starting point to achieve this goal. Whether it is a profit-seeking business – large or small – a charity or a public-sector organisation and whether you are an employee, customer, supplier, creditor, owner or just an interested onlooker, the ability to understand and evaluate accounting information is not only useful but perhaps essential if you are to survive in the harsh and competitive economic environment of today. This chapter examines the three main accounting statements (showing *profit*, *cash flow* and *balance sheet*) and suggests ways of making sense of them.

Profit

You would expect that most people, whether they have business knowledge or not, understand what '**profit**' means. Simply put, profit is revenue minus costs. However, suppose we take this very basic example of a trader's past year to see if our expectation is correct in terms of calculating profit:

> **Activity**: Harry Stoke sets up a business on January 1 with £1,000 cash, £100 worth of goods and a £500 bank loan at 10% interest. During the year he buys further goods from suppliers totalling £5,500, although at the end of the year he owed them £500 of that sum (as they gave him credit terms of a month's settlement). His sales figure was £10,000, but he, too, offered his customers a month's credit, so they owed him £1,000 at the year end. He bought a van for £900 to transport stocks and other items and paid £700 rent, £300 wages and £500 for his various other business expenses (such as fuel, heat and light and so on). He estimated

that he could afford to withdraw £50 a week for his private spending and also managed to repay £350 of the original bank loan. His unsold stock, or inventory, at December 31 was £400.

Income statement

Even with these relatively simple (and perhaps unrealistic) figures, see if you can calculate Harry's profit for the year, remembering that profit is revenue minus costs. Before we start, you must realise that there is one item in the example known as a **non-current asset** (formerly called a fixed asset), and to do the calculation properly we must estimate how long Harry intends to keep it within the business. The non-current asset is the van, and Harry bought it with the intention of keeping it for three years. We must therefore treat its annual cost as a third of its buying price. We call this allowance for wear and tear **depreciation**, in this case by the straight-line method, which is probably the simplest and most commonly used depreciation technique.

Here is a suggested profit calculation, which is properly referred to as an income statement. See how close yours is to this one:

	£	£
Sales		10,000
Opening Stock	100	
Add Purchases	5,500	
	5,600	
Less Closing Stock	400	
Cost of Sales		5,200
Gross Profit		4,800
Rent	700	
Wages	300	
Misc. Expenses		500
Bank Interest	50	
Depreciation on Van	300	
Less Total Expenses		1,850
Net Profit		2,950
Less Drawings		2,600
Retained Profit		350

Figure 3.1 Income statement for the year ended December 31, XXXX

Notice that there are three figures identified as 'profit': gross profit, net profit and retained profit. Although we didn't specify which profit we were after, the one which is perhaps most useful is the net profit of £2,950, as this is the one that is most informative about how successful, or otherwise, Harry's business is.

There are a few things to note about this answer. First is the two-column layout, showing final figures on the right and workings to the left. The leftward sequence of opening stock plus purchases minus closing stock is necessary to calculate the cost of goods sold of £5,200, shown as a final figure to the right. The resulting gross profit of £4,800 is encouraging (in that it is, indeed, a profit) but hardly surprising, as it would be a very poor business that sold its products at a lower price than it paid for them. That explains why gross profit would not have been the preferred answer to the original question of "what is Harry's profit?" The gross profit is at the end of the first stage of calculating profit, and the relevant section is known as the *trading account*.

The next section is called the *profit and loss account*. Note the van depreciation figure of £300, which is a third of the van's original cost, representing the usage of the van during the year we are looking at. If you included the bank repayment of £350 in your calculations, you should go back and look at our simple definition of profit as revenue minus costs. The repayment is neither a revenue nor a cost. Instead it is a transfer of cash back to the bank in the same way the bank transferred the £500 to Harry in the first place. The only cost involved in this transaction is the bank interest of 10% of £500, which is the £50 shown among the other expenses.

Another common fallacy is to show the *drawings* figure (meaning the amount of cash the owner withdraws from the business over the 52 weeks of the year) as one of the expenses, along with the rent, wages and shop expenses. Harry's status as the owner and sole proprietor of the business means that his earnings from the business should be treated as a deduction from the profits in the final section, known as the **appropriation account**. The final figure of retained profit (the third of our 'profit' figures) shows the portion of profit that Harry has chosen not to spend on himself but to wisely reinvest to help the business expand and grow.

So if your answer for profit differed from the £2,950 net profit shown, it is not at all unusual. We all think we understand what profit means, but specifying it exactly from a mass of seemingly random data is somewhat baffling and keeps professional accountants in business. This confusion is not helped by the fact that any calculation of profit is largely dependent on subjective judgement, as, for instance, changing the depreciation assumptions or using alternative inventory valuation methods could well produce a completely different profit figure. For this reason you should always regard the profit figure as just one possible result according to a particular set of assumptions rather than a 'unique' or 'true' indicator of business performance. And it is very different from cash flow.

Cash flow

We will proceed with the Harry Stoke example by looking at his business's cash flow, which basically means tracking any money coming in or going out of his bank account or shop till. To do this we will start with his opening position at the beginning of the year, add to it any incomings of cash from sales (the correct term for this is *receipts*) and then deduct all the outgoings of cash he made during the year (known as *payments*). By going through this sequence we should arrive at his final cash balance – the amount of cash left at the end. Note that, in this example, we mean by 'cash' the money in Harry's till and in his business bank account, added together. A steady flow of cash is essential for a business to survive, so it is vital that Harry pays close attention to this part of his business.

Again we are using the same two-column layout with final figures to the right and lists of figures requiring addition or subtraction to the left.

So, having taken into account the opening cash balance of Harry's £1,000 plus the bank loan of £500, we receive a total of £9,000 from customers during the year (made up of the £10,000 total sales minus the £1,000 still

			£	£
Opening Balance:	Harry's cash		1,000	
	Bank loan		500	
				1,500
Add Receipts:				
Cash from Sales				
(£10,000 − £1,000 owed to Harry)				9,000
				10,500
Less Payments:				
	Rent	700		
	Wages	300		
	Misc. expenses		500	
	Bank Interest	50		
	Loan repayment	350		
	Drawings	2,600		
	Purchases			
(£5,500 − £500 owed to suppliers)			5,000	
	Van		900	
			10,400	
Closing Balance				100

Figure 3.2 Cash summary for the year ended December 31, XXXX

owed to Harry), making £10,500 of total incomings during the year. All the payments or outgoings add up to £10,400, so he is left with £100 cash at the year end. Notice that the van is shown as a payment of £900, which is the amount of cash spent. The depreciation figure of £300 is not shown anywhere in the cash flow statement, as it is merely the averaging of the annual wear and tear and does not represent an actual cash payment.

Compare the cash summary to the income statement. One shows a net profit of £2,950; the other shows a cash balance of £100. The two result from very different financial statements, even though many of the figures within each are exactly the same. Perhaps the reason we all think we understand what profit is yet struggle to match the answer shown is because very few of us are used to dealing with abstract and unfamiliar details like the deferral of debtor and creditor payments, stock valuations, book valuations and provisions and so on, all of which tend to make the income statement remote and impenetrable. Even the net profit figure of £2,950 is not really visible anywhere within the business. We won't find that actual amount in the till or the bank, as it is a sort of hypothetical result on the basis that everything turns out as we have assumed. On the other hand, though, we are all very familiar with cash flow. Every day we put money in our pockets, top it up from a cash point if necessary, then spend it during the day on meals, transport and entertainment. At night when we empty our pockets, whatever we have left is the result of how much we started with, how much we added and the deduction of how much we spent. In other words, we are all accustomed to cash flow and understand inflows and outflows of money. The £100 in Harry's cash can be seen and touched and felt. It is nothing like the £2,950 profit, which is relatively ethereal and impalpable.

Balance sheet

The third main financial statement for a business or non-profit organisation is the balance sheet, nowadays known more correctly as the **statement of financial position**. This differs from the income statement and cash flow statement in that it is a snapshot or single day's record rather than an account of the whole year (i.e. the aggregate of every trading day within the year). It lists the assets acquired (meaning resources like buildings, vehicles, stock-in-trade and cash) and the liabilities (meaning outstanding bills, bank loans and owners' funds) which funded these acquisitions. As one side (liabilities) measures where the money came from and the other shows where it was spent (assets), the two sides match – hence the name **balance sheet**.

The *assets* side, on the left, distinguishes between the long-term, fixed or **non-current assets** and the short-term **current assets**. In this case the van is the only non-current asset, but if the business owned premises, machinery

Non-current Assets				Equity		
	£	£	£		£	£
	Cost	Depreciation	Net	Opening capital	1,100	
Van	900	300	600	Retained earnings	350	
						1,450
				Non-current Liabilities		
Current Assets				Bank loan		150
Inventories		400				
Trade and other receivables		1,000				
Cash and cash equivalents		100		Current Liabilities		
			1,500	Trade and other payables		500
			2,100			2,100

Figure 3.3 Statement of financial position as at December 31, XXXX

or furniture, these would also be listed along with the van. The original cost of the van is shown as £900, the depreciation accumulated so far, £300, and the net figure deducting depreciation from cost, shown as £600. To all intents and purposes £600 is what the van is worth by the end of the first year. Beneath the non-current assets are the current assets, as the running order on the balance sheet is from long-term (or illiquid) items at the top to short-term (or liquid, which means closeness to cash) items at the bottom. Current assets consist of **inventories** (unsold stocks of goods), accounts receivable (customers yet to pay for the goods Harry sold them) and cash.

Mirroring these assets are the *liabilities*, shown horizontally on the right in this case. Starting from the bottom are the short-term or **current liabilities**, meaning those that are due for repayment soon, like the bill for stocks delivered by the suppliers, who are probably expecting reimbursement within a month. Next are the **non-current liabilities**, longer-term items, in this case the bank loan. The bank originally lent Harry £500, but Harry repaid £350 of it, making the debt £150. Notice that the interest of £50 does not appear on the balance sheet at all, as it is not a liability once it has been paid (or, more likely, taken by the bank directly from the bank account).

The longest-term liability (indeed even longer-term than non-current, because it is permanent) is the owner's funds, called **equity**. The owner, Harry Stoke, contributed £1,000 in cash and £100 in inventory to the business, and this represents his equity, or capital, at the start. In addition he has generated profits during the year and left a proportion unspent, as retained profit or reserves. This reinvestment of funds has swelled his equity to a total of £1,450 by the end of the year.

The balance sheet now balances, with a total of £2,100 on both sides. The left-hand side shows a measure of the worth of the business's resources (the van, stocks, debtors and cash), and on the right it shows how much the business owes for funding these resources (to the suppliers, the bank and to Harry). Harry's contribution to the business is shown as a liability in the sense that it represents the amount owed back to him by the business. To try to make the balance sheet more memorable think of the assets side as a measure of the *resources* of the business and the liabilities side as a record of the *sources* from which these assets were funded. The assets show the monetary value of what is *owned* by the business and the liabilities side shows what is *owed*.

Interpretation

Now that we have this threefold picture of the finances of Harry's business – in terms of profitability, cash flow and balance sheet worth – we can assess its performance to judge whether he has done well or badly in his first year. The first stage of serious evaluation of business performance is *intelligent observation*. This simply means looking at every single aspect and figure and judging whether anything can be done for improvement. Is there a cost that can be reduced without actually harming eventual results? Can revenue be enhanced by doing anything differently? Sometimes it might be necessary to incur extra costs in order to add value and benefit the business, such as spending more on advertising or taking on more salespeople.

A second stage of interpretation is the technique of *ratio analysis*, taking key measures from the three financial statements in order to provide meaning to our results. A useful framework for this type of appraisal is to look at *profitability, liquidity, efficiency* and *gearing*. Financial ratio measures are most useful when we have something to compare them to, so assessing Harry's performance without reference to that of past years or competitors is somewhat limited but can still provide valuable insights.

The first stage of evaluating performance is *profitability*. While there are many organisations, like charities and public-sector bodies, which do not actively seek profit (to the extent that they even avoid using the words 'profit' and 'loss', referring instead to 'surplus' and 'deficit'), they certainly will try to avoid losses. So this is relevant to all sectors, although some may give profitability greater priority than others, according to their business objectives. One measure of profitability, taken from figures in the income statement, is the *net profit margin* (alternatively called *return on sales*): *net profit divided by sales*, and is usually shown as a percentage. You will remember that Harry's net profit was £2,950, and his sales during the year amounted to £10,000:

$$\frac{\text{Net profit}}{\text{Sales}} = \frac{£2,950}{£10,000} = 29.5\%$$

This figure, rounded to 30%, tells us that for every £1 of sales that Harry makes, 30p is pure profit. If we had comparative data for a previous year or another similar firm we could monitor the trend and make fuller judgements about business performance. The higher the profit margin, the better for Harry, although he should be aware that rivals might be tempted to undercut him to steal some of his custom.

Another area for making sense of the soundness of Harry's business is *liquidity*, or its ability to repay debt. The *current ratio* measures:

$$\frac{\text{Current Assets}}{\text{Current Liabilities}} = \frac{£1,500}{£300} = 3 \text{ times}$$

This means that Harry has short-term assets amounting to three times more than his short-term debts. So if his creditors insist on prompt payment he has a considerable safety margin to afford to pay them. Any reduction in this measure – especially if this measure dips below 1 – would affect his ability to repay his immediate debts.

There are a number of *efficiency* measures that Harry could use to measure how successful his business is so far, such as sales per employee or sales per square metre of shop space. Another useful set of ratios is to calculate the *debtor/creditor period*. By comparing:

$$\frac{\text{Debtors}}{\text{Sales}} \times 365 \text{ days} = \frac{£1,000}{£10,000} \times 365 = 37 \text{ days}$$

to

$$\frac{\text{Creditors}}{\text{Purchases}} \times 365 = \frac{£500}{£5,500} \times 365 = 33 \text{ days}$$

On average his customers are paying their bills within 37 days, but Harry is settling with his creditors at a faster rate, 33 days. This is good news for his suppliers but less so for Harry, as he is paying them before collecting money from sales. For greater credit control efficiency he could delay making payments as long as possible and do all he can to get his customers to pay up quicker.

Gearing, or *capital structure*, looks at the relative proportion of money put into the business by Harry as compared to borrowing from the bank. Borrowing should always be kept to a level that the business can afford. When Harry started the business his equity was £1,100, and his bank borrowing was £500. This works out to a proportion of 31% debt and 69% equity. By the end of the year we can see from the balance sheet, which shows £1,450 equity and bank loan of £150, that his equity has increased to 91% of net worth compared to only 9% debt. In other words, over the year he has increased his stake in the business and reduced his borrowing. This lower gearing means that he has reduced his interest payments and, if business declines in future, he will have less fear of the bank stepping in to close down the business in order to recover the loan.

Limited companies

The example of Harry Stoke is based on a sole trader running a relatively simple business. To apply the concepts of profit, cash flow and balance sheet to a larger *Ltd (private limited company)* or *PLC (public limited company)* type of business the basic principles are similar, even though the figures are bound to be much more complicated.

A limited company's income statement tells basically the same story as Harry Stoke's. Where it may differ substantially is in the appropriation account, where instead of the owner taking a share of the profits as drawings, the owners of a limited company are the shareholders, and their entitlement to profits is through **dividends**. In addition, limited companies are subject to *corporation tax*, and this deduction will also be shown in the appropriation account.

The cash flow statement for a limited company again shows outflows (the expenditure of cash, being negative, is shown in brackets) and inflows (earning cash, therefore unbracketed). However, the various activities are shown separately, as follows:

> *Operating activities*, such as income and expenditure from trading
> *Investing activities*, such as the purchase and sale of non-current assets and equipment
> *Financing activities* such as issuing shares and repaying loans

The balance sheet, or **statement of financial position**, for a limited company is laid out in **vertical** fashion rather than the horizontal style shown earlier, with the liabilities side displayed below rather than alongside the assets. Sometimes this format makes it hard to follow the asset versus liability structure shown in Harry Stoke's final accounting statement in Figure 2.3. If you are able to discern the same five sections (i.e. *non-current assets, current assets, equity, non-current liabilities* and *current liabilities*), even if they are rearranged somewhat, you will realise that the company's balance sheet is essentially the same, albeit considerably more complex.

An additional area for interpretation for limited companies is that of *stock market* or *investment ratios*. Sole traders like Harry Stoke are not quoted on the stock exchange, so it would not be possible to make sense of this aspect of their business. However, the figures for PLCs are freely disclosed and publicised so that analysts can compare measures such as earnings per share, dividend cover and price earnings ratio in order to make further judgements about their performance.

Summary

This chapter has covered:

- The three main financial statements for a business: income statement, cash flow and balance sheet.
- Ratio techniques to make sense of performance in the areas of profitability, liquidity, efficiency, gearing and investment.
- Differences between the accounts of a sole proprietor and those of a limited company.

Discussion Point 1: Describe cash flow as it applies to you, from the time you put money in your purse or pocket in the morning to the time you empty them at night.

Discussion Point 2: In what ways do cash and profit differ?

Discussion Point 3: How well does the concept of **straight-line depreciation**, which shows the loss in value of an asset evenly over its useful life, explain how your phone, car or computer declines in value?

Exercise: Look back at the Activity in Chapter 2 and see if you can prepare Barton Hill's income statement and statement of financial position from his trial balance after his first day's trading. You will need to know that his closing inventory is £1,500.

4   Budgeting

Chapter overview

Now that we have seen how past financial information is put together and analysed, the next step is to plan for the future, which is known as *budgeting*. A **budget** provides a picture or map of the resource position needed to achieve a set of objectives or to carry out a strategic plan. Budgets are vital aspects of corporate strategy in which resource requirements cascade down through the managerial layers to individual departments all the way down to the shop floor. This chapter looks at the meaning of budgeting and the steps involved in forecasting future profit, cash flow and financial position in order to ensure that all staff are doing their best for the future progress of their organisation.

Definition and reasons

A budget is an internal document or set of spreadsheets, usually compiled by the managers of an organisation to plan for the future year or beyond. The word derives from the old French 'bougette', meaning little bag or purse in which money was kept. The modern-day meaning of budget is a quantitative or financial plan set in the future to achieve certain objectives. This definition conveys three main points:

1   A budget is a *forecast*.
2   A budget is very specific in that it *quantifies* exactly what is expected to happen.
3   The purpose of a budget is to attain *objectives*, and this is the essence of why budgets are prepared.

There are many reasons firms budget, including the setting of *objectives*, *planning* and *organising* activity and *controlling* and *co-ordinating* resources. Furthermore, and perhaps even more importantly, the behavioural effects of *aligning* the expectations of all the people involved in running an organisation are very considerable. Good, clear *communication* to ensure effective *participation* and *motivation* on the part of managers and employees, *integration* of resources and *innovative vision* for the future can all be managed through successful budgetary planning.

Let's suppose that Harry Stoke, whose accounts for last year we saw in Chapter 2, wishes to conduct the next six months in a more organised way by preparing a budget.

> **Activity**: Remember from the previous chapter that Harry finished last year with equity of £1,450: a van worth £600, which depreciates by £300 a year; stock of £400; amounts owed to him by customers of £1,000 (payable in January); and cash in hand of £100. He plans to repay the £150 left owing to the bank immediately, therefore avoiding any interest. He owes his suppliers £500 and will pay this and future bills for purchases a month in arrears, aiming to buy £6,000 of stock a year in even monthly amounts. He intends to increase annual sales by 20%, offering his customers to repay evenly, month by month, on a month's credit. He will set up direct debits to pay his other bills monthly, the yearly totals being £900 for rent, £360 for wages and £840 for his various other business expenses. He estimates that with the extra income he can afford to withdraw an extra 20% for his private spending, averaging out to £260 a month. His unsold inventory is expected to be £200 at the end of June.

From these plans we can draw up budgets for Harry Stoke's business for the next half year, arranging the forecast financial information in a similar fashion to how we arranged his past accounts.

Cash budget

Perhaps the most important aspect of business planning is for the cash and bank requirements of the coming period. If Harry gets this wrong and runs out of funds at a crucial time he can be bankrupt very quickly, even if the business is potentially profitable. Here, as before, we are not too bothered about the difference between cash and bank entries, as it is the joint amount of money we need to keep track of, so the cash and bank figures can simply be added together and treated as one. We can prepare Harry's cash budget for the next six months, from January to June, on a month-by-month basis, using the same basic layout we used before:

Opening balance of cash per month
Add receipts (meaning cash in during each month)
Less payments (meaning cash out each month)
Closing balance of cash per month

Of course, the closing balance of cash for one month becomes the opening balance of the next month. In the case of Harry's payments in this example, where there is some complexity to the many outgoings Harry faces, it is useful to have a separate schedule devoted to the various entries. The sum total can eventually be transferred to the payments line in the cash budget as shown below. In this way we can forecast the exact timing of cash inflows and outflows to see how much money he needs every month.

Notice that the extra columns to the right, for summary totals and amounts owing, provide additional information to help Harry make sense of the results.

Receipts Schedule

	Jan	Feb	Mar	Apr	May	Jun	Summary	Owing
Sales	1000	1000	1000	1000	1000	1000	6000	1000
Payments Schedule								
Wages	30	30	30	30	30	30	180	
Rent	75	75	75	75	75	75	450	
Misc. Expenses	70	70	70	70	70	70	420	
Purchases	0	500	500	500	500	500	2500	500
Bank Repayment	150						150	
Drawings	260	260	260	260	260	260	1560	
Total	585	935	935	935	935	935	5260	
Opening Balance	100	515	580	645	710	775	100	
Add Receipts	1000	1000	1000	1000	1000	1000	6000	
	1100	1515	1580	1645	1710	1775	6100	
Less Payments	585	935	935	935	935	935	5260	
Closing Balance	515	580	645	710	775	840	840	

Figure 4.1 Cash budget for the six months ending June 30, XXXX (all figures in £)

Forecast income statement

Looking back at Chapter 2 we introduced the income statement with the following logical sequence:

Sales
Less cost of sales or cost of goods sold (COGS)
Gross profit
Less other expenses
Net profit
Less owner's drawings
Retained profit or reserves.

In Chapter 2 we also identified three sections:

From sales to gross profit is the record of buying and selling, known as the trading account.
From gross profit to net profit is the profit and loss account.
From net profit to retained profit is the appropriation account, showing what the owner did with the profits.

Using the same structure, Harry's budgeted income statement therefore looks like this:

	£	£
Sales		6000
Opening Stock	400	
Add Purchases	2500	
	2900	
Less Closing Stock	200	
Cost of Sales		2700
Gross Profit		3300
Rent	450	
Wages	180	
Misc. Expenses	420	
Depreciation	150	
Less Total Expenses		1200
Net Profit		2100
Less Drawings		1560
Retained Profit		540

Figure 4.2 Forecast income statement for the six months ending June 30, XXXX

Forecast balance sheet

As we saw in Chapter 3 the balance sheet is one way of measuring the value of a business, based on how much things have cost. We saw that it consisted of two main groups of items (assets and liabilities) viewed on a particular day of reckoning. Harry's forecast statement of financial position can now be prepared.

By exercising these formal plans for the future, based on the formulation of strategic objectives and realistic projections in the light of expected economic conditions, Harry Stoke has transformed his small business from an aimless, ad hoc, reactive operation into a more considered and methodical, structured and proactive enterprise. By applying the techniques of intelligent observation and ratio analysis learned in Chapter 2 Harry can scrutinise every single aspect of his business and prepare for the future with as much foresight as it is possible to have prior to actual events.

Working capital management

A thoughtful and methodical set of budgets is an important first step to ensure business survival and prolong Harry's prosperity. By looking carefully at the **working capital** of the business he can ensure that the main components are kept in check. Working capital is usually defined as current assets minus current liabilities. As we now know, current assets consist mainly of inventories, accounts receivable and cash. Current liabilities are

	£	£		£	£
Non-current Assets			Equity		
Van		450	Opening capital	1450	
(less accumulated					
depreciation of £450)			Retained profit	540	
					1990
Current Assets					
Inventories	200				
			Non-current		
Accounts receivable	1000		Liabilities		0
Cash	840				
		2040	Current Liabilities		
			Accounts payable		500
		2490			2490

Figure 4.3 Forecast statement of financial position as at June 30, XXXX

short-term creditors or accounts payable. By looking closely at these four areas the cash flow can be enhanced:

Inventories: Harry must ensure that he has sufficient stock in hand to satisfy demand and keep things ticking over. However, too much stock is expensive: it ties up funds, requires storage space and can be subject to changing fashions or spoilage. The ideal is to keep a balance between not too much inventory nor too little, which explains why **just-in-time** stock control, in which suppliers provide goods as and when needed, is so popular and successful.

Debtors: Good cash flow relies on collecting money from customers quickly. Incentives such as offering cash discounts might speed up receipts of cash, but the most effective method is also the simplest: Harry should keep in touch with his accounts receivable, invoice them promptly, follow up in timely fashion and generally be efficient in collecting what's owed to him.

Creditors: The other side of the coin is to avoid paying off accounts receivable before receiving what is due. Harry doesn't want to upset his suppliers by late payment, but he should try to agree favourable terms at the outset with the longest possible delay in paying for goods received.

Cash: Harry shouldn't rush into borrowing a fortune from the bank if it's going to put a strain on interest charges and repayments. He should look around for alternative sources of cash such as government grants, partnership or joint venture arrangement to raise money. Overall, he should ensure that cash is always available when needed, as a shortfall can quickly put an end to even the most promising enterprise.

In particular, Harry should look very carefully at the cash budget on a regular basis to make sure that all these components of working capital are constantly in check. This will ensure that *cash flow* is always under scrutiny and control to make the best of this most urgent and important of financial requirements. In the short term cash problems should be tackled by concentrating mainly on the goods or services which are earning him the most and which will get him out of trouble. In the long term everything should be reassessed to take account of changing conditions in the marketplace.

Larger organisations

The beneficial effects of budgeting are even greater in larger organisations, where the behavioural influences of budgets on staff are particularly important to bind them together with a common purpose. Budget plans are compiled in two stages, by and for all levels of management. *Subsidiary, operational* or *divisional budgets* tend to focus on each area of the business, such as sales, production, marketing, personnel or expenses, and build up a picture of financial requirements over the coming year. All these detailed estimates are then combined into an overall plan with the three elements we are now familiar with: cash flow, profitability and the balance sheet. This is called the **master budget**. These final statements, being based on subsidiary plans, cash flow forecasts, profitability projections and valuations do not just represent a complex numerical exercise but also incorporate the motivational benefits of participative ownership and participation, having – when managed properly – a far-reaching and cohesive impact on future direction.

Zero-based budgeting

A useful and interesting contrast to the usual **conventional** or **incremental budgeting** approach, which bases plans on the previous year's figures typically marked up by an appropriate percentage to allow for inflation, is **zero-based budgeting** (ZBB, alternatively known as *priority-based budgeting*). This was popularised by practices encouraged by Jimmy Carter's U.S. presidency during the 1970s and has since been commonly employed by public sector organisations, among others, wishing to plan for and accommodate future change.

ZBB takes as its basic premise the view that every pound budgeted for must be justified from scratch and all expenses are classified as new (hence the 'zero' base). Managers in an organisation that is implementing a ZBB approach usually adopt the following steps:

1 *Designation of activities:* First of all the management team conducts a thoroughgoing review of the organisation's activities, focusing on the essential purpose of the enterprise and its provision of goods or services. This exercise gives managers an opportunity to debate fresh strategic vision of the organisation's objectives and review methods of attaining them.

2 *Formulation of budgeting areas:* The overall review is then used to establish which areas need resourcing. This stage may (and indeed should) involve a complete departure from previous approaches.

3 *Ranking of budget areas:* Once the resourcing needs have been decided, the areas needing funding are ranked in order of importance.

4 *Allocation of resources:* Funds, staffing and other resources are then designated according to the chosen priorities.

5 *Monitoring:* In time, the results of the budgetary allocation are then closely scrutinised so that findings can be fed into the next round of ZBB.

The ZBB system resolves some of the major problems of the conventional budgeting approach. Instead of allowing managers to carry forward inefficiencies year after year, giving them no incentive to look for better ways of improving performance, ZBB generates a complete overhaul of current practice to drive forward change. Furthermore, whereas the traditional incremental approach makes it difficult to find funds for new schemes other than by across-the-board cuts, ZBB allows for a completely fresh strategy to be implemented to encompass changing conditions and priorities.

However, ZBB does have its drawbacks. Zero-based budgets are notoriously difficult and time consuming to prepare, requiring managers to endure much agonising and original thought. The practice can therefore degenerate into a meaningless routine and even lapse back into conventional budgeting as ideas dry up and managers revert to past routines. In any case, some ZBB decisions are marginal: much expenditure is often already committed as a result of decisions made in the past.

Summary

This chapter has covered:

- The definition and purpose of budgeting.
- How to piece a master budget together to forecast cash flow, profit and balance sheet.
- How working capital management can maximise cash flow.
- The behavioural influences of budgeting within large organisations.
- Zero-based budgeting.

Discussion Point 1: Define the word 'budget' in relation to your chosen organisation.

Discussion Point 2: Why do organisations budget? Can you think of reasons budgeting is unnecessary? Discussion with colleagues may widen your views, especially if they have practical experience of budgeting.

Discussion Point 3: Think about the budgeting system or process within an organisation. Do the managers involved generally understand the budgeting process? Are the budgets realistic in relation to the organisation's forecasts and to its environment? Are the budgets properly discussed before they are set in motion? Are budgeting decisions made on the basis of complete information? Are there any negative outcomes of following budgets rigidly?

Exercise: Stapleton Services plc is a consultancy firm which has just declared its annual balance sheet as follows (in £00):

Non-current Assets	Cost	Dep	Net
Land and buildings	12,000	2,000	10,000
Office furniture	3,000	1,000	2,000
Motor vehicles	6,000	4,000	2,000
	21,000	7,000	14,000
Current Assets			
Inventories		500	
Accounts receivable		2,000	
Cash and bank		4,000	
		6,500	
Current Liabilities			
Accounts payable		500	
Corporation tax		1,000	
Dividend proposed		1,000	
		2,500	
Net current assets			4,000
			18,000
Equity			
10m ordinary shares			8,000
Reserves			4,000
			12,000
Non-current Liabilities			
Bank loans at 10%		4,000	
Debentures at 5%		2,000	
			6,000
			18,000

The company's plans for the coming year are:

1 The expected earnings will be based on 100,000 hours at £200 an hour. All transactions are on credit, with a debtors collection period averaging 36 1/2 days.
2 The direct costs arising from the service are expected to be £40 an hour.
3 The administration costs will be £5m, including £600,000 for depreciation on buildings, £300,000 depreciation on office furniture and £100,000 depreciation on vehicles. The general expenses are expected to be £6m.
4 Commission to agents will be 10% of turnover.
5 The loan interest will be paid during the year, but no repayments will be made to the lenders.

6   25% of last year's year-end debtors will be written off.
7   At the year end the stocks are expected to be £500,000.
8   The creditors figure shown above is 25% higher than the budgeted figure for next year.
9   Corporation tax is 20%, payable in the year following.
10   The dividend will be 8p, payable in the year following.

Required

Produce the budgeted statements for profit, balance sheet and cash flow for next year.

5 Cost classification and behaviour

Chapter overview

Organisations cannot stand still. They have to respond to the demands of the marketplace and to the threats and opportunities presented by the competitive environment. Change – in systems, products, services, market approaches, operational technologies, human resource strategies – is a principal and necessary factor in the quest for success conducted by today's enterprises. And, naturally, implementing change costs money.

All the management activities concerned with planning, implementing, monitoring and controlling the efficient use of systems and the processes of change in organisations have cost elements associated with them. When managers put their budgets together, they try to forecast the likely scale of the sacrifices they will have to make. Financial management seeks to control and reduce expenditure, comparing actual costs against forecasts and taking action to minimise outgoings.

In this chapter we will look at the various types of costs which organisations incur and go on to examine some ways in which managers can improve their understanding of the related issues and provide answers to the essential question of what it's going to cost.

Classifying costs

When managers make decisions they have to look carefully at the alternative courses of action that are open to them and assess all aspects of each option. In order to do this efficiently they need to analyse the relevant cost implications. Until they know how much Plan A or Plan B is likely to cost they cannot reliably predict how much profit each plan will generate for their enterprise. One of the most important control systems used in any organisation is one that tracks, analyses and assigns costs, comparing real-life experience with budget forecasts.

As we have already seen in previous chapters, there are several different categories of cost or expense. Here are some of the expenses that are likely to occur, according to the type of financial account in which they appear.

When a firm makes rather than buys the product it goes on to sell, it lists the costs of production in a *manufacturing account*. These 'factory' costs are typically the **direct materials** and **direct labour** associated with actually making the product and the *overhead* or **indirect costs** such as supervision and power.

The *trading account* records the gross profit made by comparing sales of goods or services to the cost of purchase or manufacture of those items.

The *profit and loss account* presents the organisation's net profit. It includes the rest of the expenses, such as administrative costs, selling costs, finance costs and research and development expenditure.

The *appropriation account* shows what the owner or owners choose to do with the resulting profit or loss.

Fixed and variable costs

Managers responsible for planning and paying expense budgets will be aware that some costs increase as activity varies, and others remain static. They will look to divide expenses into those which vary significantly with production volume and those which do not. In cost accounting a traditional distinction is made between fixed and variable costs. The crucial difference between these terms involves the relationship between the cost being considered and the level of *output* or *activity* in the organisation. A **variable cost** is one which increases as more production or activity is undertaken, such as the raw materials cost for a manufacturer. A **fixed cost** remains constant regardless of the level of activity, such as the rent payable on the premises occupied.

Looking back at some of the costs classified already, we can now consider which are fixed and which are variable. Note that some costs can come into both the fixed and variable camps, and others depend on the sector or the kind of organisation in which we are working, so it will be difficult to make a firm decision in some cases.

- *Raw materials* are clearly variable, as the more goods we produce, the more materials we need with which to make them. Incidentally, remember that we are looking at the total cost increase rather than the cost per unit, which may become cheaper with bulk buying.
- *Direct labour* is also a variable cost, as we need to employ more people (or pay overtime) as production increases. The best example is where workers are paid 'piece rate' for each item produced. However, it is commonplace in many firms for productive wages to have a basic

component, paid just for turning up (hence a fixed cost), regardless of output. So an expense can be made up of both fixed and variable costs: such an expense is called a *semi-variable cost.*

- *Supervision* is most likely to be a fixed cost, as it comprises a salaried payment, although it is quite possible to include bonuses or productivity payments, which are variable.
- *Maintenance* can be either fixed or variable. If equipment is maintained according to usage – such as when a company's vans or trucks are serviced every 10,000 miles – it will be a variable cost. If maintenance is carried out, say, every six months regardless of how frequently the vehicles have been in use, it is a fixed cost.
- *Depreciation* is most commonly calculated on the basis of the expected life of the non-current asset – for example over a three-year lifespan on a straight-line basis – so in this case it is a fixed cost.
- *Power*, such as electricity driving heavy machinery, is most often regarded as a variable production overhead. Even this is not clear cut, as part of a gas or electricity bill includes a standing charge, which is a fixed payment levied regardless of the amount used.
- **Purchases**, or more correctly the cost of goods sold, is a variable cost, as it increases with the volume bought.

Most of the remaining profit and loss charges are usually regarded as fixed – certainly *administration costs* (which is often comprised mainly of staff salaries), *financial expenses* (interest on borrowings) and *research and development* (laboratory staff salaries). The exception is perhaps *selling and distribution costs*, which can include sales force commissions and delivery charges and hence could be variable.

Activity: Consider the items of expenditure in the following list according to (a) whether they constitute capital or revenue expenditure, (b) which account they should appear in (either manufacturing, trading, or profit and loss account), (c) what category of cost they are (such as direct materials, direct labour, direct expenses, production overhead, administration overhead, selling overhead, distribution overhead, finance overhead or research overhead) and (d) whether you consider the item a fixed, variable or semi-variable cost:

purchase of a delivery vehicle, plastic for product, machine depreciation, lighting and heating, buildings insurance, product royalties, bank interest payable, machinists' wages, telephone charges, managers' salaries, electricity, cleaners' wages, sales force remuneration, stationery, laboratory equipment, machine lubrication oil, canteen costs, vehicle maintenance, scientists' salaries.

As a guide, here are some suggestions:

- Purchase of delivery vehicle – **capital expenditure.**
- Plastic for product – revenue expenditure, manufacturing account, direct materials, variable cost.
- Machine depreciation – revenue expenditure, manufacturing account, production overhead, fixed cost.
- Lighting and heating – revenue expenditure, split among all departments (hence features in manufacturing and profit and loss account), fixed cost.
- Buildings insurance – revenue expenditure, split among all departments (hence features in manufacturing and profit and loss account), fixed cost.
- Product royalties – revenue expenditure, manufacturing account, direct expense, variable cost.
- Bank interest payable – revenue expenditure, profit and loss account, finance overhead, fixed cost.
- Machinists' wages – revenue expenditure, manufacturing account, direct wages, variable cost.
- Telephone charges – revenue expenditure, profit and loss account, administration overhead, semi-variable cost.
- Managers' salaries – revenue expenditure, profit and loss account, administration overhead, fixed cost.
- Electricity – revenue expenditure, manufacturing account, production overhead, variable cost.
- Cleaners' wages – revenue expenditure, split among all departments (hence features in manufacturing and profit and loss account), fixed cost.
- Sales force remuneration – revenue expenditure, profit and loss account, selling overhead, variable cost (if commission based).
- Stationery – revenue expenditure, profit and loss account, administration overhead, fixed cost.
- Laboratory equipment – capital expenditure.
- Machine lubrication oil – revenue expenditure, manufacturing account, production overhead, variable cost.
- Canteen costs – revenue expenditure, split among all departments (hence features in manufacturing and profit and loss account), fixed cost.
- Vehicle maintenance – revenue expenditure, profit and loss account, distribution overhead, fixed cost.
- Scientists' salaries – revenue expenditure, profit and loss account, research overhead, fixed cost.

Don't worry if you disagree in some cases, as several of these items can fall into different categories, depending on opinion or organisational practice. As long as you can explain and justify your position, alternative answers are acceptable.

Other ways of classifying costs

The differentiation of fixed, variable and semi-variable costs is not the only method of cost classification. Other possible categories are:

- *Direct or indirect costs* – depending on whether a cost can be attributed specifically to the production of a good or a service.
- *Controllable or non-controllable costs* – depending on whether a cost is under the direct control of a manager or department.
- *Avoidable or unavoidable costs* – depending on whether a cost is the result of a deliberate management decision, such as entering a new market, for instance, or one that would have to be incurred in any case.
- *Opportunity costs* – measure the sacrifice involved when selecting one course of action over another.
- *Sunk (or committed) costs* – costs which have already been incurred and cannot be recovered.
- *Incremental (or differential) costs* – the additional cost of extra activity.

Summary

This chapter has covered:

- Cost classifications for different types of corporate expenditure.
- The definition of fixed and variable costs.

Discussion Point 1: Can you identify the fixed and variable costs in your chosen organisation?

Discussion Point 2: In general, how successful has your organisation been in stabilising or reducing costs?

Discussion Point 3: What aspects of cost management is your organisation (a) good at? (b) bad at?

Exercise: The organisers of a concert are trying to decide between two venues for their next event. They expect to have a full house for whichever theatre they eventually choose.

The Hippodrome Theatre is the larger of the two, seating 5,000 people at a charge of £20 a head. The Royal is more luxurious, so £25 per head can be charged for its 3,000 seating capacity. Hire costs are the same at £1,000 for each venue, but the Hippodrome requires additional insurance provision to cover the higher numbers, at a cost of £2,000.

The equipment being used for organising the event cost £4,000, with depreciation at £1,000 for the period of use. Administrative and other costs come to £6,000. The Hippodrome is farther away, so extra travel and accommodation costs arising from its use will amount to £12,750. The additional travelling time means that if the Hippodrome is used, the organisers will have to cancel an alternative event expected to raise around £800.

Printing and materials for the event amount to £8,000, apart from the free programme to be given to each member of the audience, at a cost to the organisers of £2 per programme. Publicity and promotion are likely to cost £1,800.

Required

a   Calculate the costs of holding the concert at either of the two venues.
b   Advise the organisers which theatre provides a greater financial benefit and how knowledge of fixed and variable costs can help them with their decision making.

6 Break-even analysis

Chapter overview

In everyday management talk 'breaking even' means much the same as 'surviving'. When managers agree that they were lucky to break even on a particular project they mean that one or two more ventures like that could easily ruin their company. Nevertheless, apart from its colloquial use, the break-even concept is a constructive and valuable one which accountants and financial managers can use in a positive way to identify practical business needs and objectives. This chapter considers how managers can use this concept as an analytical business tool for decision-making and problem-solving tasks. We'll also look at its shortcomings and difficulties.

Predicting levels of activity

Break-even analysis, alternatively called cost volume profit analysis, uses the distinction between fixed and variable costs which was the subject of Chapter 5 to make forecasts of the levels of activity required to embark upon a business venture and survive – or even make a profit.

> **Activity**: Suppose Ivy Bridge is running a small business and selling an item which costs £6 for a price of £10. Her weekly fixed cost is £200 for rent. How many goods does she have to sell in a week to break even?

It's fairly easy to see that by selling 50 items her revenue will be £500 and her costs will also be £500 (made up of 50 items at £6 each = £300 plus the £200 for rent). She has made neither profit nor loss, hence has broken even.

There are a number of ways of defining the **break-even point**. One view is to regard it as the point at which we are making neither profit nor loss. Another definition is that it is the point where total costs (i.e. fixed plus variable) equal total revenue (units sold times price).

The break-even formula

The formula Ivy used for deriving the break-even point in units is:

$$\frac{\text{fixed costs}}{\text{selling price per unit} - \text{variable cost per unit}} = \text{break-even units}$$

Figure 6.1 Break-even formula (units)

In Ivy's case her fixed cost of £200 divided by the £4 she makes on the sale of each item tells her that she must sell at least 50 items to pay the rent. The denominator of this formula (the selling price minus the variable cost) is called the **contribution**, as every time a unit is sold for £10 it contributes £4 towards paying off the fixed costs, leading eventually to profit.

A third way of defining the break-even point is to consider it from the view of contribution. This is admittedly a rather unusual way of looking at it, but it can be quite useful in some circumstances. If we regard Ivy's contribution of £4 every time she sells an item for £10, or 40p for every £1 of sales, we can see that the contribution is a kind of profit measure. Break-even occurs when the total contribution (£4 multiplied by 50 items sold) equals the fixed costs. We can express this 40p per pound as a 40% *profit-volume ratio*. This gives us a second way of finding the break-even point, this time shown as a monetary figure rather than a number of units.

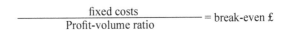

$$\frac{\text{fixed costs}}{\text{Profit-volume ratio}} = \text{break-even £}$$

Figure 6.2 Break-even formula (£)

For Ivy this gives £200 divided by 40%, a break-even cost and revenue figure of £500.

An even simpler way of working out the break-even £ figure is to multiply the break-even units of 50 by the price of £10, which again gives a result of £500.

Determining profit

We can use break-even theory to calculate anticipated profit. If Ivy is optimistic that she will do more than just break even and aims to make £100 profit on top, she can vary the formula in Figure 6.1 by adding this expected profit to the numerator of the equation shown. So if she adds the £100 to the £200 fixed costs and divides the sum by the £4 contribution, she can work out that she needs to sell 75 items to achieve her required profit level.

Avoiding a loss

When the market is sluggish and Ivy's optimism is unfounded, harsh measures may be called for. She may wish to pitch her prices at the very lowest level to offload all her goods without making a loss. Here again the break-even concept is useful. Can you work out at what price Ivy can afford to sell all her stock of 100 items without making a loss?

You can find the answer by rearranging the break-even formula in Figure 6.1. Since you now know the number of units (100) but not the selling price:

The fixed cost of £200 divided by 100 units gives you £2.

So Ivy needs to make a contribution of £2 on each item (which means selling them at £8 each) to leave the market without making a loss.

The break-even chart

The usual way of showing the break-even concept visually is with a *break-even chart* or *graph*. All the functions are straight lines because of the simple assumptions we have been making, especially the idea that variable costs increase exactly in proportion to units sold. Units sold are shown on the horizontal (x) axis, with costs and revenue in £ on the vertical (y) axis. We are back to our original weekly plan of selling items costing £6 at a price of £10.

The easiest way to understand each function is to consider each end of the scale, from 0 units to the maximum number of 100 items. The fixed costs of £200 are constant throughout, as the rent is £200 when sales are zero and still £200 even if Ivy sells the lot. The variable costs range from £0 when nothing is sold to £600 if she sells everything. Add the two together and we get a total cost line ranging from £200 at no units to £800 at the maximum level.

We can now tell what the profit is at the maximum capacity of 100 units sold, a figure of £200 (made up of total revenue of 100 × £10 minus the total costs of £200 rent and £600 for the units). We can calculate profits at any level of sales, either by measuring the gap between costs and revenue on the graph or calculating the figures. Any sales level below the break-even point of 50 items will be at a loss.

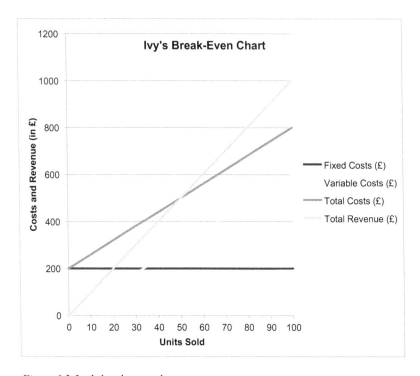

Figure 6.3 Ivy's break-even chart

Limitations of break-even analysis

Some of the conventional problems with break-even analysis arise largely from the simple assumptions used. Costs are all considered as straight-line functions when, in reality, variable costs often become cheaper as savings from bulk buying and economies of scale reduce unit costs. Similarly, fixed costs, which are considered to be constant at all levels, may well increase as activity increases.

Total revenue is also oversimplified, as it too is plotted as a straight line, taking no account of demand theory, which states that quantity demanded is likely to fall as price rises.

The analysis described is perfectly satisfactory for a single-product firm or for planning a one-off event. But difficulties arise when we consider multi-product companies with a diversity of variable costs. Furthermore, how can fixed costs be split among various products? The answer is to regard the 'package' of items produced as if it were a single unit, considered in ratio proportion to each item's output. This type of analysis might produce results in due course but is inevitably rather clumsy and unworkable.

Remember, too, that break-even analysis is only as reliable and accurate as the data and assumptions used.

The role of costing

Knowledge of an organisation's costs is extremely important for managers wherever they work, especially at a time when enterprises attach such a high priority to cutting back on expenses and remaining competitive. Understanding which costs are fixed and which are variable, always identified in relation to output or activity, is the first step towards exerting control over these costs. The contribution approach, which depends on knowing the variable cost per unit of the good or service delivered, also gives an important 'bottom line' figure, which is invaluable in negotiations with clients.

By understanding the implications of cost volume profit approaches and studying the application of break-even techniques, managers will be able to make the most of their opportunities in the market.

Summary

This chapter has covered:

- How the analysis of fixed and variable costs can help determine break-even and profit-making strategies.
- How to prepare a break-even chart and use break-even formulae.
- Some problems with conventional break-even techniques and assumptions.

Discussion Point 1: In what ways is break-even analysis unrealistic?

Discussion Point 2: What types of business are best suited to using break-even analysis? Which are the worst?

Discussion Point 3: Which assumptions about fixed and variable cost make break-even analysis difficult to apply in practice?

Exercise: Speedwell is a small business selling a type of safety equipment for road vehicles. Monthly rent, administration and depreciation costs total £3,000. The item costs £65 to make and sells for £75. Graph and calculate Speedwell's break-even chart and break-even point.

7 Marginal and absorption costing

Chapter overview

The approaches to costing used by managers in organisations must be practical, realistic and equitable. The costing techniques that they employ must be reliable and efficient. Additionally, today's highly competitive corporate environment calls for costing approaches to be comprehensive; managers must calculate the costs of a product on the basis of grouping all the various related production and operational costs – fixed, variable and semi-variable – and categorising every relevant cost-centre activity in the business. In this chapter we will examine the ways in which managers can use marginal and absorption costing techniques to address their business objectives and meet competitive challenges.

The significance of cost issues

Managers often carry out performance audits to monitor the achievements (and under-achievements) of their organisations. These exercises, in which costing considerations can play a vital part, focus on corporate strengths and weaknesses, typically addressing the need for remedial action to tackle inadequate performance or considering the measures required to improve a problematical market position.

Fundamentally, because organisations are commonly required to generate profits for their shareholders – or at least to operate efficiently and break even – the task of ensuring that their operational activity is most effectively and economically harnessed to their corporate objectives is a key management concern. Cost issues are particularly significant in this context.

Analysing costs

Activity: Nailsea Niknaks make seaside souvenirs. They are currently producing 1,000 products a week at a cost of £10 each. The market retail price is £11. New management wishes to make full use of spare capacity and increase market share by turning out 2,000 units a week. Market research suggests that if the company is to sell everything, the retail price has to fall to £9 per unit. What questions would you ask of the firm's managers, and how would you respond to their wishes?

Were you tempted to resist their plans for expansion in the knowledge that a loss would be inevitable? Or would you have reluctantly agreed but resigned yourself to using poorer-quality though cheaper materials or taken other painful cost-cutting measures? Then perhaps you hadn't looked closely enough at the firm's costs or asked the right questions.

To assess the situation properly we need to find out how the £10 cost figure was derived. Suppose the answer, based on the current production run of 1,000 units, is:

	£
Direct materials	3,000
Direct labour	2,000
Variable overheads	1,000
Fixed overheads	4,000
Total	10,000
Hence the unit cost is £10.	

We now need to ascertain which are the fixed costs and which are the variable costs.

• The **prime costs**, materials and labour, are normally regarded as variable, on the assumption that the workforce is paid according to hours worked or units produced rather than receiving a basic level of pay.
• The *variable overheads* cover items like power, maintenance and other indirect costs, which increase as more is produced.
• The **fixed costs** include such items as rent, supervision, administration and straight-line depreciation.

So, assuming that direct materials, direct labour and variable overheads vary exactly with output – in other words, if production doubles then each variable cost also doubles – and that the fixed overheads remain constant even when production expands, we can now compare the two alternatives.

Profit or loss?

At the 1,000 activity level Nailsea Niknaks make a profit of £1,000, calculated as 1,000 units selling at £11 each (making £11,000 revenue) minus costs of £10 each item times 1,000 (making £10,000 costs).

At 2,000 units, instead of making a loss, as you may have inferred when told that an item costing £10 to make would be sold at £9, the firm will actually increase profits, making £2,000. The revenue is now 2,000 units × £9, making £18,000. And the costs of doubling output are:

	£
Direct materials	6,000
Direct labour	4,000
Variable overheads	2,000
Fixed overheads	4,000
Total	16,000
Hence, profits of £2,000.	

Marginal and absorption costing

The Nailsea Niknaks example highlights the significance of variable (sometimes called marginal) and fixed costs in managerial decision making.

The figure of £10 for total cost per unit is actually misleading when considering other capacity options. Yet surprisingly, many firms produce exactly this type of information and expect managers to make sound decisions. It is referred to as an *absorption cost* figure and is calculated by adding together, or absorbing, all the costs (fixed as well as variable) of producing 1,000 units and dividing by the number of units. At the 2,000 units level the absorption cost suddenly reduces to £8 per unit (£16,000 divided by 2,000 units). Using an absorption cost figure derived from a different production level can mislead rather than help.

A far more meaningful way to approach this type of problem is by concentrating on the marginal (or variable) cost per unit, by ignoring the fixed costs. In the 1,000 unit situation the marginal or variable cost per unit is £6 (£6,000 divided by 1,000 units). In the 2,000 unit situation the answer is again £6 (£12,000 divided by 2,000 units). This £6 figure excludes the fixed costs and is therefore unaffected at different levels of production.

Using the contribution approach

There is another way of working out profitability which we can apply to Nailsea Niknaks. Remember the *contribution approach* from the chapter on break-even analysis?

With the marginal cost figure of £6 in mind we can assess the two options much more quickly by using the contribution per unit as a guide:

The contribution per unit is the selling price of £11 minus the marginal or variable cost per unit of £6. This gives £5.

At 1,000 units, the £5 contribution per unit times 1,000 units amounts to a total contribution of £5,000.

Deduct the fixed costs of £4,000, which we haven't taken into account yet, and we have the £1,000 profit figure.

In the expansion situation we have a contribution of £3 per unit (£9 − £6).

£3 times 2,000 units − that's £6,000.

Take away the fixed costs of £4,000 and we have the £2,000 profit figure.

So the contribution approach can be used by a busy non-financial manager to show that profits will be higher, saving the lengthy and arduous calculations of revenues minus costs that an accountant would normally use to tackle the problem. In fact we can refer to the contribution approach as the 'manager's way' of looking at a production comparison and the more conventional revenue-minus-cost approach as the 'accountant's way'.

The qualitative side of decision making can be equally important to the quantitative results. For instance, a deal which doesn't make much money but allows entry into new markets, offers foreign trade advantages, gains a prestigious client, allows use of new equipment for other purposes or gives environmental benefits may be chosen regardless of the financial outcomes.

Summary

This chapter has covered:

• The meaning and importance of the terms '**marginal costing**' and 'absorption costing'.
• Using typical managerial and accounting approaches to solve profitability issues.
• Awareness of the financial (quantitative) and non-financial (qualitative) factors in the choice of corporate strategic options.

Discussion Point 1: What arguments favour marginal costing as a basis for pricing a good or a service?

Discussion Point 2: What arguments favour absorption costing as a basis for pricing a good or a service?

Discussion Point 3: Think of other factors apart from financial viability which might influence a manager's choice of possible options for adopting a business proposal.

Exercise: Fishponds Ltd make garden water features. If the coming year is as normal, their costs are expected to be:

	£
Materials	80,000
Labour	90,000
Variable production overhead	10,000
Fixed production overhead	30,000
Administration expenses	12,000
Selling expenses	8,000
Sales are expected to be 10,000 units at an average price of £250 each.	

Assume that materials, labour and variable production overhead are all variable costs, with the rest being fixed costs, and that the company has considerable spare capacity. Two independent enquiries are made to make use of this capacity, both requiring extra production:

Option A: A large firm wishes to use Fishponds as a subcontractor to supply an additional 1,000 units for which they will pay £190 each. This will entail no increase in fixed costs.

Option B: Another firm is offering the higher price of £200 per unit for 1,000 extra units. In order to fulfil this contract, Fishponds will need to acquire a special machine costing £50,000. The machine will require extra running costs of £11,000 a year and is expected to last for five years.

Decide whether Fishponds should accept one or both offers, or just stick to their normal activities.

8   Overhead recovery

Chapter overview

We have seen how marginal costing aids managerial decision making, by considering the variable costs alone. Fixed costs should not be forgotten, though, particularly with regard to pricing policy, where overhead costs have to be recouped and reflected in the final price. The term *overhead recovery* or *overhead absorption* refers to the way these fixed costs are 'recovered' or 'absorbed' into the price. This chapter explains the concept of overhead recovery and demonstrates its significance for sound financial management, providing some practical examples.

The overhead problem

Overheads – the great majority of which would normally be classified as fixed costs – are incurred as a matter of course as part of a business's overall operations. So when managers have to put a price on a single product, such as a light bulb for instance, they have to ensure that the price of that item reflects not only the direct material and labour costs incurred in making it but also the indirect costs such as rent, rates, depreciation, maintenance, administration and so on. Consider the problem of taking all these costs into account when arriving at a selling price for a single light bulb if you are the factory manager.

a   A very simple approach to overhead recovery would involve dividing the total overhead costs incurred by the business for a period by the total number of units produced during that period. This approach is fine if the business only produces light bulbs of a single design and specification. However, if it (more realistically) makes a range of products such as electrical switches, sockets, plugs, junction boxes and so on, requiring different manufacturing assembly or packaging times, charging the same amount of overhead to all items would clearly be unfair and inefficient.

b   An alternative approach would take this time difference into account. By dividing the total overhead cost by the total number of production hours worked it is possible to calculate an overhead rate per hour. This is a more reliable approach than A, but it may still be less than satisfactory because some departments of the business – for example, those containing more expensive equipment or having to pay higher maintenance or rental charges – are likely to be more costly to run than others.

At this stage it is worth noting that overhead recovery, the process whereby overheads are charged to cost units, can use a variety of types of absorption rate – such as labour hour rate, machine hour rate or using a percentage mark-up factor as a multiplier – depending on the type of product offered and the production methods employed.

Activity: Vinney Green is a carpenter operating from a workshop near his home, producing items to order, such as cabinets and tables. He has completed a request to make a bedroom wardrobe and records the costs in order to invoice the customer. His material costs of wood, glue, screws, etc. are catalogued accurately, coming to £36. His labour is also fairly easy to keep track of, as he has made a note of the 8 hours it took him to craft the wardrobe during his 40-hour week. Comparisons to similar tradespeople show that £8 an hour is a reasonable rate so he charges £64 for direct labour. The hardest part of the exercise for Vinney is deciding how to cost the overhead accurately in order to charge the client. Instead, he decides to apply a mark-up of 50% over and above the sum of his direct material and labour costs in order to give himself plenty of room to recoup overheads and make a profit.

The need for an accurate way of charging for overheads is shown here, with Vinney using a rather random and arbitrary 50% mark-up to estimate indirect costs and leave him with a profit. The calculation therefore becomes:

	£
Materials	36
Labour (8 hours @ £8 per hour)	64
Total prime costs	100
50% mark-up	50
Bill to customer	150

Vinney is happy with this and looks forward to receiving payment of £150 for the job. However, as we shall see in the next section, a more detailed knowledge of overhead recovery may well have been to his benefit.

Costing A-words

Allocation means charging costs which are clearly identified, such as, in this case, the materials and labour. There is no doubt that the materials and the eight hours' worth of labour belong to this job alone, so Vinney is very confident in allocating a total of £100 to the client for these prime costs.

However, Vinney is not confident about the rest of his bill, with the 50% mark-up amounting to little more than a guess. If he actually itemises all his overheads he will find that the list is probably longer than he originally thought. It includes rent, rates, telephone, insurance, vehicle use, gas, electricity, water and all the other little and large things that he needs to spend to run his business. The great majority of overheads are fixed costs and, by definition, fixed costs do not relate to a particular item he makes in his workshop. Overheads occur whether he produces anything or not.

In some cases, such as running the van, Vinney needs to separate his private use from his business use, and this is where the second A-word, **apportionment**, comes in. There are several different ways of calculating how much he drives his van for work rather than leisure, such as on the basis of time or mileage. He may conclude that, since he uses the van twice as much for the business as for the home, a $\frac{2}{3}:\frac{1}{3}$ split is fair. So he calculates van depreciation, fuel, road tax, insurance and the like and apportions two-thirds of the total as a business overhead. Any reasonable method is acceptable, so you may find that apportionment in some businesses may be worked out on a completely different basis to that of another, but both are equally valid.

Once he has identified and totalled up all the overhead costs for the business, he can apply the third A-word, *absorption*. Suppose the weekly overheads for the business come to £480. We have already seen that Vinney's average working week is 40 hours. He can use what is known as a labour hour rate, calculated by dividing the total overhead of £480 by his direct labour hours of 40 hours to give a figure £12 per hour. This is not to be confused with the labour hour rate he charges of £8 per hour. The £12 is the amount he must charge customers per hour, merely to recoup the £480 worth of overheads incurred during the week. So the overhead cost associated with making the wardrobe works out to 8 hours worked multiplied by £12 for each of those hours, a total of £96. Added to the £100 materials and labour costs, Vinney needs £196 just to break even!

We can now see that Vinney's original bill of £150 would not even pay for the prime costs and overhead incurred during the time he made the cabinet, let alone leave him with a profit. A few more costings like this and he will soon be out of business.

Overhead recovery in larger organisations

Our small-business example has parallels in larger organisations. The steps used by Vinney to cost the results of his carpentry endeavours are similar to those employed in many larger, well-known enterprises.

Cost allocation, apportionment and absorption are seen as suitable methods for costing and pricing their products and services and have been in use since the Industrial Revolution and Victorian times. However, this traditional way of working out how much something costs, and therefore how much it should sell for, has been overtaken in recent years by a practical alternative known as activity-based costing (ABC).

Summary

This chapter has covered:

- The meaning of the term 'overhead recovery'.
- Simple overhead recovery calculations based on operational data.
- The use of overhead recovery in small and large organisations.

Discussion Point 1: See if you can find out more about how costing and pricing are carried out in your selected organisation.

Discussion Point 2: Suppose you are splitting costs between your department and another one. What possible bases for apportionment can you think of?

Discussion Point 3: What are the disadvantages of using a single overhead rate based on labour hours when costing a product?

Exercise (Part One): Rangeworthy Ltd produces clocks and has two departments, with overhead expenses as follows:

	Manufacturing Dept (£)	Assembly Dept (£)	Total (£)
Supervisors' wages	1,000	1,000	2,000
Indirect labour	2,000	1,000	3,000
Rent and rates			9,000
Power			3,000
Repairs to machinery	1,500	1,100	2,600
Depreciation on machines			900
Supplementary information			
Direct labour hours	10,000	25,000	35,000
Machine hours	2,000	3,000	5,000
Floor area (sq mtrs)	20,000	10,000	30,000
Book value of plant	£10,000	£8,000	£18,000

Question 1

a   Use the supplementary information to apportion the three missing costs (i.e. rent and rates, power and depreciation) between the two departments.

b   Calculate (i) the labour hour rate and (ii) the machine hour rate, for each department. Assume that the first three overheads named relate to labour and the last three to machine.

Part Two

One of the clocks made, called the Whitehall, incurred the following costs for the production of 500 units:

	Manufacturing (£)	Assembly (£)	Total (£)
Materials	200	100	300
Labour	300	600	900

The direct labour hours worked on the Whitehall amounted to 1,000 in Manufacturing and 500 in Assembly. The machine hours worked were 400 in Manufacturing and 600 in Assembly.

Question 2

Using the overhead rates calculated in Question 1(b), calculate the overall cost of each Whitehall made.

9   Activity-based costing (ABC)

Chapter overview

We have seen how overheads are normally recovered by linking them to direct hours worked – even though the two are not always connected. In the1980s two American academics, Robert Kaplan and Robin Cooper, queried this relationship. They felt that basing the treatment of overheads, which are primarily fixed, on labour or machine hours provided convenient arithmetic but took too little account of how the costs included were incurred. The commonly accepted overheads/direct hours connection was, in their view, a spurious one.

Nowadays, direct labour hours make up only a small proportion of organizational costs and machine hours comprise a much smaller one, even in manufacturing enterprises. Fixed costs dominate most organisations' cost structures, and this dominance – in an age when managers are trying every trick to reduce expenses – needs a far better explanation than the simple assertion that fixed costs are not affected by the volume of production.

This chapter examines the use of activity-based costing, an approach which seeks to establish a more reliable and representative basis for tracking and controlling costs.

Identifying cost drivers

The key to the ABC approach is to identify the **cost drivers** of the activities of a business – in other words, the activity-related factors that generate the business's costs. Think of the various activities associated with the materials used in a manufacturing business, such as storage for instance. The physical volume of materials stored is likely to be a main driver of warehousing costs and, as such, is a driver of storage overheads. ABC subjects all the factors affecting overheads to close analysis. The everyday use of information technology and computers to collect, store and analyse data has made this more possible.

If the number of goods produced doesn't cause fixed overheads to go up then what does? Or in the case of the goods received in order to assemble a finished product, if it's not the sheer number of items causing indirect costs to rise, then what does affect them? Perhaps it's the number of suppliers rather than the number of components, as each supplier has to be dealt with separately. So if only one supplier provides a whole host of items, then the cost of arranging and paying for them is far more controllable than if many different suppliers were involved. Thus the number of suppliers is the cost driver, not the actual number of units ordered.

In order to adopt ABC, every aspect of fixed cost has to be scrutinized in order to identify the cost driver for that particular business activity instead of simply classifying it as a fixed cost and therefore unexplained and uncontrollable.

Activity: Let's look again at the case of Vinney Green from the previous chapter. He calculated an overhead absorption rate of £12 per labour hour, based on weekly overheads of £480 divided by 40 hours worked per week, and applied that rate to every hour worked on an item in order to recoup his overheads. Vinney now wants to apply the principles of ABC to see if he can use the technique to his advantage. He thinks carefully about how his overheads are incurred and comes to the conclusion that about £100 of the £480 is related to telephoning and delivering to customers.

So the activity of maintaining contact with his customers is a **cost driver**, and telephone and travel bills form a common **cost pool**, both linked to the same cost driver. If he has 10 customers in a week his phone and petrol bills are 10 times as much than if he has only one customer because of the frequent visits and phone calls required. Vinney now realizes that his overheads are reduced when he has only one customer to deal with and only one delivery to make and are significantly increased when he has to go all around town to keep a number of clients happy.

Of course, this is an over-simplification and a considerable stretch of the imagination, but the upshot is that, on this basis, he can trace a part of his overhead to each customer rather than thinking of it as a constant lump sum of £100 a week. In fact, a simple sum of £10 per customer per week (£100 phone and delivery overhead divided by 10 customers) might emerge from his calculations. The ABC concept helps Vinney think of fixed overheads as more manageable and controllable. Indeed, he may be tempted to see advantage in taking a large order from a single customer as compared to smaller orders from a variety of diverse patrons, even if the total number of items is the same. This is the basis of ABC calculations, which can become quite complex when a number of overhead categories and cost drivers are considered.

The future of ABC

Since it emerged in the 1980s as a way of addressing the problems caused by distorted or unreliable costing information, activity-based costing has attracted a good deal of attention and has gained many supporters and adherents. It not only helps financial managers calculate their costs more accurately but provides them with a useful tool for managing and controlling overheads. ABC is becoming increasingly influential in the area of cost management, enabling the collection and analysis of information on the significant resource-consuming activities of an organization. Areas such as design, research and development, marketing and distribution, production and servicing can be examined in detail to focus managers' attention on the underlying causes of expenditure and should lead to a deeper understanding of longer-term cost-management approaches.

Summary

This chapter should help you:

• Explain the ABC approach in simple terms.
• Understand the concept of cost drivers of business activities.
• Outline the advantages of ABC and explain why many businesses find this approach attractive.

Discussion Point 1: What constitutes an 'activity' for the purpose of identifying cost drivers?
Discussion Point 2: List the principal cost drivers in the activities of your chosen organization.
Discussion Point 3: Would the use of ABC lead to a more accurate pricing policy?
Exercise: Hotwells offers two services, X and Y, using specialist staff. The annual demand is 1,000 customers requiring X and 2,000 for Y. The method of absorbing the overheads of £700,000 according to specialist labour hours established the following costs for each provision of the service:

	X £	Y £
Specialist labour (based on a rate of £20 per hour)	80	100
Overheads (based on a rate of £50 per labour hour)	200	250
Total	280	350

As a result X was priced at £350 and Y at £400.

Question 1 Explain how the overhead rate of £50 per direct labour hour was arrived at.

Question 2 Prepare a statement to calculate Hotwells' overall profits, showing the profits for X and Y separately.

The new management team wishes to apply a more thorough method for charging the overheads, using an activity-based costing approach. The overheads are examined more fully, and the following figures are discovered in relation to the two services:

	X	Y	Total £
Administration	9 staff	6 staff	200,000
Promotion/liaison	9 staff	1 staff	200,000
Buildings, etc.	70%	30%	300,000

Question 3 Use activity-based costing principles to reallocate the overhead costs between X and Y.

Question 4 Prepare a new profit statement, showing X and Y separately.

Question 5 Compare the two approaches. Comment on your findings and especially on the pricing policy.

10   Performance measurement

Chapter overview

Performance measurement is an important aspect for any organisation, whether it is a corner shop, a government department or a huge multinational corporation. An effective monitoring system to record and analyse achievement has several advantages: it helps establish the current position, as compared to competitors or the past; it communicates direction to employees and customers; it influences behaviour to do things right for the future, stimulating action to correct areas of weakness; and it facilitates learning, promoting understanding of how the organisation functions.

The balanced scorecard

The current approach to performance measurement has been popularised by two American academics in the form of the 'balanced scorecard'. *Robert S. Kaplan* is a teacher, consultant and author, professor of accounting at Harvard Business School, and the founder of activity-based costing, a method of accounting for overhead which has revolutionised many company costing systems and is dealt with in Chapter 9. Formerly dean at Carnegie-Mellon University, he has a master's in electrical engineering and a doctorate in operations research. In 2006 he received the Lifetime Achievement Award from the American Accounting Association. His partner in developing the scorecard is *David P. Norton*, a consultant and author who founded the Renaissance Strategy Group and set up the consultancy Nolan, Norton & Co., later acquired by KPMG. His own background was also in electrical engineering, although he went on to study for a doctor of business administration at Harvard, where the two met.

Four perspectives

Kaplan and Norton give the analogy of an aeroplane pilot needing to keep an eye on the many dials and indicators in the cockpit in order to fly successfully. Over-reliance on any one type of measure, such as profit for instance, can divert attention from another problem area and eventually lead to trouble. Their four areas of concentration are:

* financial (how do we look to the stakeholders?)
* external customers (how do they see us?)
* internal process (what must we excel at?)
* innovation and learning (can we continue to improve and create value?).

The *financial perspective* is probably the most obvious and well known, comprising measures such as cash flow, profitability, sales growth, market share, gearing and so on along the lines demonstrated in Chapter 3. But the authors' point is that this one way of measuring alone is insufficient to maintain an integrated view of the overall performance of the organisation and that the three other areas are just as important in an ever-changing environment. The *customer perspective* looks at delivery times, key accounts, percentage of sales from new products, enquiries translating into sales and so on. The *internal business perspective* measures cycle times, unit cost and a host of specific measures aimed at efficient product or service delivery. The *innovation and learning perspective* examines the organisation's training and staff development procedures, the introduction of new products, and the abilities of personnel to deal with change and to cope with future needs.

The 'balance' in the title of the scorecard can be interpreted in several ways. There should be a mixture of financial and non-financial measures, some drawn from the past and some that help predict the future. Short-term objectives and goals should be addressed as well as long-term strategic direction. External customers and owners are considered as well as internal processes. Soft aspects like customer perceptions and image are every bit as valuable as hard measures like return on investment or market share.

Key performance indicators

For an organisation to devise its own scorecard, using the four key perspectives devised by Kaplan and Norton, the outset is to know exactly what the organisation is trying to achieve in terms of a clear strategy and objectives. If an initial goal is survival, then a financial measurement can be based on cash flow, a customer measure can focus on retaining clients and so on. Although it is important that the system is (and is seen to be) driven by senior management it must involve all levels of staff for it to be carried out with conviction, with full discussion taking place at all stages. A set of qualitative as well as quantitative measures should be designed as a means of embracing the objectives set. About four **key performance indicators (KPIs)** in each of the four categories is probably a good starting point, making 16 in all. Guidelines for effective performance indicators might be that they are:

- feasible – capable of quantification and easy to measure
- relevant – appropriate to what is being measured
- valid – well based
- reliable – a trustworthy guide to what is being measured
- timely – up to date
- meaningful to users – applicable at all levels
- appropriate across range – high and low readings should have validity
- repeatable – results show consistency
- balanced – a mixture of diverse measures across the board.

Once devised, the indicators should be implemented into a regular reporting system. Results should be carefully scrutinised, with action taken to make all staff aware of progress and to improve the measures. Target and actual figures should be compared to promote knowledge and action and benchmarked against other leading organisations to see how their standards are attained. Throughout, the system should be constantly reviewed to ensure that it is achieving its original objectives and that it is kept up to date.

Once the balanced scorecard is in place it can be used to drive change, transforming the culture of the organisation according to the newly set objectives. The variety of soft and hard indicators can identify trends in the changing nature of business even before they manifest themselves into final results, perhaps avoiding problems before they take root.

Activity: Clifton, a business consultancy, has the following facts and figures relating to the last two years:

	This year	Last year
Number of clients	*430*	*395*
Consultants	*70*	*63*
Support staff	*57*	*50*
Training expenditure (£)	*100,670*	*99,670*
Revenue from fees (£)	*5,590,879*	*4,890,804*

You are required to devise some key performance indicators (KPIs), using the four balanced scorecard perspectives, for a presentation to Clifton's senior management. Interpret the results.

Starting with the *financial perspective*, it is possible to calculate revenue per client by dividing revenue from fees by the number of clients. Therefore, last year's figure of £12,302 has risen this year to £13,002, an increase of just over 5%. Certainly, an increase in revenue per client suggests that the business is on an upward path.

Turning to the *customer perspective*, one possible measure might be to look at the number of clients dealt with per consultant by dividing the former by the latter. A fall from 6.27 to 6.14 suggests that the consultants are not seeing as many of their clients as last year, but be careful when it comes to interpretation. Making sense of the figures is the most important part of the exercise, but it can vary according to who is analysing the KPIs and what their objectives are. On the one hand we might see this 2% drop as bad for the consultancy business, as our experts are not managing to get around to their customers as before. However, it can equally be seen as a positive aspect, as consultants may be devoting more time and attention to each client. This may be the reason our revenue has gone up, as clients are paying more for improved service. There are often two sides, sometimes even more, when it comes to interpreting results, so always think carefully about how to rationalise them.

An *internal perspective* can be obtained by considering the number of support staff per consultant. An almost 3% rise, from 0.79 administrators per advisor to 0.81, suggests that each consultant is being served better by back-up staff. Others might say it implies inefficiency or overemployment of second-tier workers.

The final consideration is *innovation and learning*. If we take the training expenditure and divide it by all staff (we are not told whether it is spent on consultants or support, so add both together), we see a 10% fall from £882 to £793. Do you see this as a useful cost saving or a failure to keep staff informed and updated?

The Clifton example shows that even from limited data it is possible to devise a useful set of KPIs. However, interpreting them should always be done with deliberation and with an awareness of how others might discern alternative perceptions.

Summary

This chapter has covered:

*   The Kaplan and Norton balanced scorecard and its four perspectives.
*   Guidelines for effective key performance indicators (KPIs).
*   Illustration of how KPIs can be devised and interpreted.

Discussion Point 1: How do key performance indicators (KPIs) help evaluate performance?

Discussion Point 2: A hospital wishes to monitor performance by setting up a balanced scorecard with the usual four perspectives. Discuss possible measures they might use within each area.

Discussion Point 3: Devise KPI measures to show whether you and your colleagues are performing efficiently.

Exercise: Using data from the Clifton activity, can you think of different KPIs for each of the four balanced scorecard areas?

11 Standard costing and variance analysis

Chapter overview

'Variance', in accounting terms, refers to the degree to which an actual figure in a corporate financial statement differs from a budgeted or forecast figure – for example, the gap between the cost of a product or service incurred and the cost originally anticipated. **Variance analysis** is therefore concerned with recording, explaining and assessing the difference between forecast data (as contained in the budget) and the actual results which occur. It combines the advantages of looking at future performance with the benefits of benchmarking against the recent past, therefore providing the basis of a very effective management control system.

This chapter gives particular attention to the technically detailed form of variance accounting called *standard costing*, which is used in the manufacturing industry, local authorities and other sectors engaged in repetitive or batch process production or services. It is important to keep in mind the important aspects of management behaviour which the practice of this technique should encourage, such as communication, employee motivation and participation and the integration of teams and departments as well as the more efficient numerical and financial practices which it facilitates.

Standard costing

In sectors where operations take place in a fairly short cycle and quick feedback on costs is needed – for example, those engaged in mass or batch production – cost estimates have to be regularly compared to actual costs, typically on a weekly or monthly basis. Such estimates are called **standard costs**. The standards in question are established on the basis of the predicted prices of materials, labour and overheads for the relevant control period. Rapid cost feedback enables managers to spot variations from these estimates and to bring about corrective action well before the end of the conventional accounting period.

The procedure for standard costing consists of five basic steps:

1   Set the standards.
2   Record the actual costs.
3   Calculate the variances.
4   Analyse the variances.
5   Take appropriate action.

We can look at each individual stage and consider the implications for management.

1   *Setting standards*: It is vital that standard costs for materials, labour and overhead are assessed accurately and that the resulting standards are attainable with reasonable effort. If they are set too high, ideal standards can end up demotivating shop floor workers who cannot match the performance expected of them and give up. The reverse is also true. If minimum standards are too easily attained and can be accomplished without effort, the employees have little incentive to work harder.
2   *Recording actual costs*: Managers need to have a quick and accurate reporting system to compile and feed back the actual results for comparison with the budgeted standards.
3   *Calculating the variances*: The variances are calculated showing the overall difference between standard and actual items and broken down in more detail to show the individual components as sub-variances. They are identified as *adverse* if they are more costly than budgeted and *favourable* if savings result.
4   *Analysing the variances*: At this stage managers need to explain the quantitative variances which arise from this exercise in qualitative terms if they are to understand where the problem is and how steps can be addressed. Furthermore, they should use this analysis to identify who or what is responsible for any shortfall so that it can be corrected.
5   Taking appropriate action: This is the most important outcome of a standard costing system for managers, as effective measures are needed to remedy the cause of the variance. Remember that it is counterproductive to rush into immediate action without working out all the possible implications of what we are doing. Apparent solutions can all too often lead to further problems if not carefully thought out. To illustrate standard costing and variance analysis, take the example of Lawrence Weston:

Activity: Lawrence Weston is a joiner making tables. Lawrence expects to use 2 metres of wood per table, at £10 a metre, so the standard cost of materials per table is £20. Lawrence subsequently calculates his actual usage of wood over the past month and it averages out to 3 metres a table at £9 a metre, a total of £27.

Materials variances

The *total materials variance* is therefore £7 Adverse or £7A. This can be broken down further into sub-variances according to *price* on the one hand and *usage* on the other.

Materials price variance: The standard or expected price of wood for Lawrence's tables was £10 per metre, but the actual price turned out to be £9. This £1 difference represents a cost saving, so it is favourable. Multiplied by the actual units used (namely, 3 metres per table) the materials price variance is therefore £3 Favourable or £3F.

Materials usage variance: The standard usage of wood per table was 2 metres and the actual usage 3 metres, and adverse variance of 1 metre. Multiplied by the standard price of £10, this makes a materials usage of £10 Adverse or £10A.

Note that the two sub-variances, price at £3F and usage of £10A add up to the overall variance of £7A to provide a useful check figure.

Identifying and correcting adverse results

Now that the variances have been calculated they need to be explained and corrected. Many **exception reporting** systems that use such techniques concentrate only on the adverse variances, the usage in this case, as they appear to be more likely to be the root of the problem. Lawrence's usage of 3 rather than 2 metres per table could have been for a number of reasons: inefficient methods, lack of training, poor tools and working conditions, lack of incentives and so on. It is the manager's job to try to identify and remedy the adverse results. On the other hand the favourable price variance could have been caused by astute or timely purchasing by whoever was responsible for supplies, so they clearly deserve a pat on the back. However, if inferior-grade materials were bought cheaply, this seemingly favourable initiative may well have contributed to the unfavourable usage – not such a praiseworthy move after all.

A similar approach can be applied to labour and overheads, so that a set of variances can be calculated for all the costs of a process. Ally these results to the same sort of exercise for the revenue side and we have an invaluable, detailed control system with which to analyse the profit of the firm overall.

Calculating variances

Here we show all the variance calculations for a standard costing system, with the overall variance at the top of the pyramid and the sub-variances below. The object here is to classify variances as adverse or favourable rather than positive or negative, with costs which are more than budgeted being adverse. On the revenue side of the equation is the sales or income variance and its two sub-variances of price and volume. Variances resulting in less income are adverse and those boosting turnover are favourable.

Advantages and disadvantages of variance analysis

Using the approaches demonstrated in this chapter, every aspect of costs and income can be carefully scrutinised, with each variance studied carefully to

Materials
TMV = SC – AC

MPV = (SP – AP) × AU   MUV = (SU – AU) × SP

Labour
TLV = SC – AC

LRV = (SR – AR) × AH   LEV = (SH – AH) × SR

Fixed Overheads
TFOV = AFO – (AH × SRph)

FOExV = AFO – BudgFO   FOVoV = (AH × SR) – (BudgH × SR)

Income
TMgV = SI – AI

IMgPV = (SP – AP) × Avo)   IMgVoV =(Svo – Avo) × SP

A = actual	I = income	SRph = standard rate per hour
C = cost	L = labour	T = total
E = efficiency	M = materials	U = usage
Ex = expenditure	Mg = margin	V = variance
FO = fixed overhead	P = price	Vo = volume
H = hours	S = standard	

Figure 11.1 How variances are calculated

assess its overall effect on profits. Detailed variance analysis can therefore be seen to offer the following advantages:

1 *Management by exception*: Exception reporting focuses on the largest adverse variances first and seeks to correct the inefficiencies highlighted by such a control system. Favourable variances should not be neglected, as they too require explanation.

2 *A yardstick for comparisons*: Comparing past results with projected results yields useful insights, especially if feedback is swift and covers a short timescale, thus being more identifiable by those responsible.

3 *Targets for efficiency*: A standard costing system can be used to encourage behavioural benefits to staff by generating useful targets, performance indicators and other measures.

4 *Consideration of costs*: Since variance analysis requires timely and detailed examination of the whole range of costs it can lead to further economies and provide scope for cost-cutting and other beneficial initiatives.

5 *Rationalisation of price*: Closely allied to the investigation into costs is the scrutiny of pricing policy in the light of findings from the standard costing control system.

6 *Accountability*: The results of variance analysis translate into a very specific path of responsibility where individual, group or policy failings can quickly be identified, informed and corrected.

7 *Speed and simplicity*: Once implemented, variance analysis is clear and can be reviewed according to a short and regular cycle of a month or even less.

However, a variance system does have some disadvantages, too.

1 *Implementation and maintenance*: It can be difficult and costly to set up a detailed standard costing system and keep it going effectively.

2 *Inaccurate and misleading standards*: If the standard costs are erroneously set, the task of correcting mistakes can be time consuming and may distract and demotivate employees.

3 *Bureaucracy*: Such a system leads to a great deal of extra paperwork which staff might find unnecessary and threatening, typically seeing it as something that keeps them from doing what they feel is their real job.

4 *Blamelaying*: An authoritarian organisation can use such a system to apportion blame for mistakes on the part of its staff. Even in a more relaxed environment people could feel that such intricate recording methods may be used against them, so they may be tempted to play it safe and avoid risks.

Summary

This chapter has covered:

- The stages of standard cost procedures and variance analysis.
- Standard costing for materials, labour, overheads and income, showing variances and sub-variances and their classification as adverse or favourable.
- Advantages and disadvantages of a standard costing system.

Discussion Point 1: Does variance analysis provide a useful management control system, or does it make people think someone's looking over their shoulder or take attention away from their real jobs?

Discussion Point 2: Would a strict variance system make staff avoid taking risks?

Discussion Point 3: What do you consider a variance analysis system's main advantages and disadvantages?

Exercise: Ashton District Council – a local authority – uses a standard costing system linked in with its budgets for its street cleaning and refuse collection service as follows:

Budget for year	£	£
Income: 20,000 miles of cleaning at £5 per mile		100,000
Direct materials: 1,000 kg at £7 per kilo	7,000	
Direct labour: 5,000 hours at £5 per hour	25,000	
Fixed overheads	35,000	
		67,000
Budgeted Profit		33,000

Note that the budgeted fixed overheads are charged on the basis of direct labour hours: £35,000/5000hrs gives a fixed overhead rate of £7 per direct labour hour.

Actual results for year	
Income: 18,000 miles of cleaning at £6 per mile	108,000
Direct materials: 1,200 kg at £6 per kilo	7,200
Direct labour: 4,500 hours at £5.50 per hour	24,750
Fixed overheads	41,000
	72,950
Actual Profit	35,050

Calculate the variances and use them to reconcile the two profit figures.

Calculation of variances

	Key
Materials (M):	T = total
TMV = SC − AC	S = standard
	A = actual
MPV = (SP − AP) × AU MUV = (SU − AU) × SP	C = cost
	P = price
Labour (L):	V = variance
TLV = SC − AC	U = usage
	R = rate
LRV = (SR − AR) × AH LEV = (SH − AH) × SR	H = hours
	E = efficiency
Overheads (O):	Vo = volume
TOV = AO − (AH × SRph) SRph = standard rate / hour	
	Ex = expenditure
OE × V = AO − BudgO OVoV = (AH × SR) − (BudgH × SR)	

---

12   Responsibility accounting

Chapter overview

One major outcome of the general trend towards business reorganisation which has affected so many enterprises in recent years has been a considerable degree of corporate decentralization. This tendency is often seen as a recent development, but its origins can be traced back to the 1950s when the U.S. General Electric Corporation set up separate parts of its organisational structure as *strategic business units* (SBUs). The intention was to give additional strategic and financial management responsibility to each section of a large organisation instead of letting the firm operate as a single, large, unwieldy mass.

The move towards decentralization has important implications for financial management generally and for costing in particular. Charging costs to products across an entire organisation is seen by some as inefficient and incompatible with effective cost control because it cannot accurately pinpoint areas of responsibility. In this chapter we will examine the system known as responsibility accounting, which seeks to trace costs and revenues to the people or departments that have incurred them.

Responsibility accounting and responsibility centres

Decentralisation often makes sound strategic sense when an organisation decides to diversify, perhaps in search of new markets. The most significant benefit of decentralization is financial: it is simply better to improve corporate accounting practice by defining the cost and revenue responsibilities of unit managers and monitoring their performance than to have the central financial function try to sort out the whole company's cost problems. Hence the argument for responsibility accounting and responsibility centres.

Responsibility accounting seeks to attribute costs and revenues for a particular unit or department to the individual manager or team of managers who are accountable.

A *responsibility centre* is an area or segment of an organisation in which a single manager or team of managers is answerable for that division's financial performance.

Four degrees of responsibility

Several degrees of responsibility are possible, but a broad twofold split into **cost centres** and **profit centres** is commonly used. Here, though, we'll highlight four degrees of responsibility, extending from the least powerful type of centre to the one with the most authority.

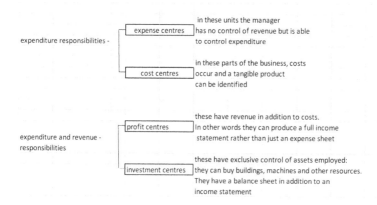

Figure 12.1 Responsibility centres

The responsibility centre ethos

The first two types of centre are those commonly referred to as **cost centres**, and the last two are generally referred to as **profit centres**. Each one is a step further on from the previous one in terms of decentralized control, breadth of autonomy and managerial accountability for expenses or revenues, extending to capital investment responsibility where they can buy expensive items of equipment.

The underlying philosophy holds that each individual segment of the organization behaves like a separate business unit, with buying and selling between divisions and **key performance indicators** (KPIs) such as turnover and profit being calculated for each section. In this way each person in that centre will be more interested, involved and motivated than if they were operating within what they might see as a large, impersonal institution.

Responsibility and authority

One of the most important tasks of the central financial function in an organisation that is implementing a responsibility accounting system is to issue regular performance reports in order to ensure that the managers of responsibility centres are kept up to date on how well they are sticking to their budgets (or deviating from them) and that senior management remains fully aware of any variances. It is vitally important that all differences between budgeted costs and actual costs are recorded in these reports so that the causes of differences can be pinpointed and corrective action taken.

However, the system will not operate efficiently unless the individuals who are charged with the responsibility for incurring costs have the necessary authority to control them. Problems may arise where the responsibility for certain expenses is shared – in the case of raw materials costs, for example, where both operations and purchasing management are likely to be involved. Another important task of the central financial function will therefore be to help define and correlate areas of departmental authority within the corporate management structure.

> **Activity**: Rodway Ltd is a service provider incurring the following annual costs: Department A (18,000 hours of work, payable at £40 per hour) or £720,000; Department B (15,000 hours, payable at £30 per hour) or £420,000; and fixed costs of £500,000. On the revenue side, the full, or combined, service (involving one hour of Department A's work and one hour of B's) is charged out at £100. Department A also supplies 3,000 hours of work to outside firms at a price of £60 an hour.

To calculate Rodway's profitability for the year:

		£
Revenue:		
3,000 hours of A's service at £60 per hour		180,000
15,000 hours of combined service at £100		1,500,000
Total revenue		1,680,000
Costs:		
18,000 hours of A at £40 per hour	720,000	
15,000 hours of B at £30 per hour	450,000	
Fixed Costs	500,000	
		1,670,000
Profit		10,000

Figure 12.2 Rodway's profit

Rodway's profitability is £10,000, with both departments co-operating to make a contribution to the firm.

However, a reshuffle applies the responsibility approach to the two departments, A and B. They will each become separate profit centres, sharing fixed costs equally. The department heads have agreed a transfer price of £50 for the sale of A's services to B. The profitability of each department now becomes:

	Dept A		Dept B	Total
Income (3,000 hours at £60)	180,000			
(15,000 hours at £50)	750,000			
	930,000	(15,000 at £100)	1,500,000	2,430,000
Costs (18,000 hours at £40)	720,000	(15,000 at £30)	450,000	1,170,000
		(15,000 at £50)	750,000	750,000
Fixed Costs (half of £500,000)	250,000		250,000	500,000
Profit	(40,000)		50,000	10,000

Figure 12.3 Departmental profits

We can see that Rodway is still earning a profit of £10,000, but Department A seems to be loss making, while B appears to be bailing the company out by making profits over and above A's losses.

The impression that B is making up for A's shortcomings is actually determined less by its apparent efficiency and more by the decisions of setting the transfer price and sharing the fixed costs. Different values of each will still result in a profit of £10,000 overall but will simply shift the proportion of profit between the two centres. Sometimes responsibility accounting is used to make judgements about performance when in fact managers should really focus on a fair establishment of the terms of the deal.

When responsibility accounting goes even further by allowing departments to take their own initiatives in order to increase profitability, events can backfire. If, for example, profit centre managers find cheaper providers outside their own company, they may be able to enhance their own profitability while damaging that of the partner department, whose sales collapse as a result.

Three principles of responsibility accounting

The three important principles that senior management should keep in mind when planning to implement a responsibility accounting system are:

1   There should be goal congruency – in other words, clear correlation and harmonization of objectives – between the departments or

divisions of the organisation. Section managers should not seek to implement policies which are harmful to the rest of the enterprise.

2   Each section should be viewed as autonomous in accounting terms. Its profits should not depend on the performance of other departments.

3   If the departments of the organisation are to be assessed under a responsibility accounting system, such assessments should be reliable judgements of their performance rather than of the financial aspects of the corporate reorganisation (that is, factors dependent on the transfer pricing and allocation of fixed costs).

Summary

This chapter covered:

- The meaning of the term 'responsibility accounting'.
- The differences between the various types of responsibility centres.
- How responsibility accounting is practiced in a typical service or manufacturing organisation.

Discussion Point 1: What distinguishes profit centres from cost centres?

Discussion Point 2: What are the advantages and disadvantages of organising work groups into responsibility centres?

Discussion Point 3: Why is profit not always an appropriate measure of divisional performance?

Exercise: Downend is a service-based business, incurring the following costs:

Department A (16,000 hours payable at £30 an hour)	£480,000
Department B (12,000 hours payable at £25 an hour	£300,000
Fixed costs	£400,000
Total costs	£1,180,000

The full, or combined, service (involving 1 hour of work in A and 1 hour in B) is charged out at £90. Four thousand hours of A's services alone are sold to outside firms at a price of £50 an hour.

a   Calculate Downend's yearly profit, before the company implements a responsibility approach.

Try using the contribution approach as well to arrive at the same answer.

b Now apply the responsibility approach to the two departments by making A and B separate profit centres, sharing fixed costs equally. The heads have agreed a transfer price of £45 for the sale of A's services to B. Calculate the profits of each centre.

Again, use the contribution approach to arrive at the same answer.

c Suppose now that a new competitor enters the market, offering a service similar to A's for only £40 an hour. The head of department B wishes to hire the competitor, as this will substantially reduce his costs. The head of department A is concerned that, as she is unlikely to offer her service to outside firms, her own department's profits will be seriously affected. Consider the implications of the new competitor from the point of view of each division and for Downend as a whole.

13 Investment appraisal

Chapter overview

Those in an organisation who have investment centre responsibility of making major acquisitions lasting for years, such as buying machines, vehicles, buildings or even other businesses, need to have some way of assessing whether such a large-scale investment is worthwhile. The equipment being considered could be as small as a mobile phone or as large as a battleship. **Investment appraisal** (sometimes called project appraisal or long-term decision-making) techniques provide a financial guide as to whether such a plan makes economic sense.

This chapter considers four methods for making such an assessment, two fairly simple and obvious ones which anyone can remember and use as a preliminary estimation as to whether to proceed. The other two techniques are rather more complicated and rely on a concept called **discounted cash flow**. Fortunately, nowadays, spreadsheets allow us to calculate projects at the touch of a button.

The ingredients

In order to make a financial assessment of a long-term project we need to have certain information. In fact, since the venture is mainly in the future we have very little known information at the outset, so most of the figures we require have to be, of necessity, guesswork. This may in some cases be a type of educated guesswork, where we have done something similar before or when we are pretty certain of the outcomes, but in all cases we are trying to predict the future. The information we need is:

- The initial cost of the equipment or project
- The receipts and payments likely to occur as a result
- The lifetime of the project

- The cost of capital
- The residual value of the equipment at the end of its use

As you can see, the only item in the list known at the outset is the *initial outlay*. In the case of major projects, such as building a football stadium, information technology systems, aerospace projects or oil and gas extraction, the eventual cost often turns out to be much higher than originally forecast, so even this 'known' factor may well be a completely different figure to that originally projected.

Taking the second ingredient listed, you will realize by now that the *receipts and payments* refer to cash flow, or cash in and cash out. The reason that we use cash flow to measure the financial results of the intended project is because, as we saw in Chapter 3, cash can be a far more reliable measure than its alternative, profit. Cash flow is a unique and verifiable figure, whereas profit depends on assumptions like depreciation rates and inventory valuations, a combination of actual income and expenditure as well as book valuations and other imputed figures. As such, given so much uncertainty with the figurework, cash flow provides a more certain basis for foundation than profit. Calculating the net cash flow arising from incomings and outgoings of cash is probably the hardest part of setting up the figures, but it is crucial in determining the project's success or otherwise.

Even the relatively simple task of assessing how long a project will last is harder than it sounds. If the project involves the purchase of a machine it could conceivably be operative for anything from 2 to 15 years. For a building or oil exploration project it could be much longer. Most organizations have an in-house policy through which they assign a set life to each type of equipment for doing the investment appraisal sums.

The next item on the list is the cost of capital, and this refers to the interest rate relating to the funds used to finance the project. This could simply be the rate charged by the bank for borrowing the money used to pay for the project.

Finally, the **residual value** is the amount recoverable if a machine, for example, is sold off at the end. Nowadays, in these environmentally conscious times, it may be necessary to pay for disposing of items responsibly, so this may be a negative rather than positive cash flow, shown at the very end of the project's life.

Activity: Blaise's Bakery is considering the purchase of a cake-making machine to automate production. The machine will cost £10,000, with Blaise borrowing the money from the bank at 8% p.a., and is likely to last 5 years. Blaise estimates that, once she has taken into account the extra cash outgoings of electricity, training and maintenance, her additional sales of cakes and lower staffing costs will give her a surplus of £3,000 for each of the 5 years. She will scrap the machine for nothing at the end of the 5 years.

Now that Blaise has made her projections, we can show her project profile as follows:

Year	Net Cash Flow (£)
0	−10,000
1	3,000
2	3,000
3	3,000
4	3,000
5	3,000

Note that in the first year, we differentiate the beginning of the year (Year 0), when the machine is bought and the project is under way, from the end of the year (Year 1), by which time the machine will have earned Blaise a net cash inflow of £3,000. Similarly, by the end of Years 2, 3 and 4 a further £3,000 is estimated to have been earned by the end of each year. In Year 5 another £3,000 is forecast, and the machine will have been disposed of at neither cost nor gain.

Simple techniques

We can now apply a couple simple investment appraisal techniques to advise Blaise whether the machine is worth buying. They are simple in that they are both fairly intuitive, and they don't require complex calculation as in the discounted cash flow techniques we will be looking at later.

Payback

One way of assessing the project is to calculate how long it will take Blaise to get her £10,000 investment back. As she anticipates that she will get a surplus of £3,000 each year, then after 3 years she should get a total of £9,000 back. So in the fourth year she will be on course to get the remaining £1,000 after the first third of the year. So her **payback** will be in 3 years and 4 months, or 3⅓ years, or 3.333 years. The quicker she gets her money back the better.

Accounting rate of return (ARR)

The next method of assessing the project has a variety of forms, some involving profit rather than cash flow. For simplicity, and since these 'simple techniques' are meant to be intuitive and memorable, a rather unusual version of *ARR* is presented here. The intention is to provide Blaise with a percentage measure of return for her to compare with the 8% interest she is paying the bank. So if she focuses on the total of 5 years' worth of £3,000 (i.e. £15,000) in proportion to the £10,000 cost of the machine, she will be getting a return of £5,000 overall. This works out to 50%, divided by 5 years, making 10% a year. So the ARR of the project seems to exceed the interest rate of her loan, suggesting that buying the machine may well be to her advantage.

Both these methods are somewhat rough and ready, so Blaise would be wise not to stake her life savings solely on the result of Payback and ARR. However, they do act as a useful guide to financial viability, and they have the additional merit of working together in tandem. Payback rewards those projects which return their outlay more quickly, and ARR prefers those with a higher overall return. So alternative projects which pay back quicker but don't earn as much in total will have a worse ARR. Or others which earn more in aggregate but delay returns until later years will have a longer payback. In this way, Blaise can compare other uses for her £10,000 to arrive at her preferred decision.

Discounted cash flow (DCF) techniques

In order to understand the more complicated *DCF* methods we need to appreciate the significance of the interest rate to the value of money over time. Now, this is not a reference to *inflation*, which has the effect of raising the money value of goods year by year. For example, house prices are now much higher than they were 50 years ago because of inflation, but the intrinsic utility of the product, the house, is the same. It is only the money measurement (perhaps a few thousand pounds then and hundreds of thousands now) which has changed. For the purpose of this analysis we will ignore the effects of inflation and assume it to be 0%.

The interest rate being referred to in DCF calculations is the cost of capital, meaning what the percentage rate is of the funds being used to finance the project. In Blaise's case the rate is 8%.

To illustrate how this interest rate can be understood, suppose you were offered a choice of £100 now or £100 in a year's time. Given such a choice most people would plump for £100 now. This is a wise choice, not only because you have the opportunity to get your hands on the money immediately – indeed, who knows if the offer will still be valid in a year, or where you might be in the future? But there is another reason for having the £100 now, and that is because you could invest it in a bank and earn interest on it as from today. To delay for a year will lose you the chance of a year's interest. This is the rationale that banks use with your savings, offering you a reward for putting your money in a bank rather than spending it. To calculate:

£100 at 8% will mature into £108 over the course of a year. In 2 years it will become £116.64 and in 3 years £125.97.

This is the principle of *compound interest* and is based on a formula of:

$$FV = PV(1 + r)^t$$
FV = Future Value, PV = Present Value, r = the rate of interest
and t = time or the number of years

So if PV is the £100 and r is 8% (0.08 when shown as a decimal) in the first year (t = 1) the formula gives £108.

In the second year (t = 2) the amount will grow to £116.64 and in the third (t = 3) £125.97.

So compound interest can be calculated for any monetary amount at any rate of interest over any period of time using the formula above. It provides a way of measuring the value of money over time, because if you were now offered nearly £126 in 3 years' time rather than £100 now, you may be tempted.

Discounted cash flow relies on the same formula, rearranged to make:

$$FV = \frac{PV}{(1 + r)^t}$$

By using this formula, which now shows Future Value as the isolated term, we can apply it to Blaise's Bakery at the rate of 8% to show the time value of money.

We now realize that the future cash flows of £3,000 differ from one another, in that the first is more valuable than the second, and so on, because each gives us an extra year to earn interest. In the first instance, £3,000 is the Present Value. Dividing it by $(1 + r)^t$ or $(1.08)^1$, which is 1.08, gives £2,777.7 recurring, or £2,778 when rounded to the nearest whole number. In fact, £2,778 can be proven to be the Present Value of £3,000 because it will become £3,000 in a year if invested at 8%.

The second year's £3,000 divided by $(1.08)^2$ or (1.08×1.08) or 1.1664 gives £2,572.016. If invested for two years at 8% it, too, will become £3,000. Notice that the more distant these amounts of £3,000 are over time, the less valuable they become when discounted (which explains why the word 'discounting' is used).

By discounting each cash inflow according to the formula we get:

Year	Net cash flow (£)	Discounted cash flow (£)
0	−10,000	−10,000
1	3,000	2,778
2	3,000	2,572
3	3,000	2,381
4	3,000	2,205
5	3,000	<u>2,042</u>
		NPV <u>1,978</u>

This is the principle of DCF, reinterpreting future values of £3,000 to their present values, assuming an 8% interest rate. Of course, the initial £10,000 cost of the machine does not need to be discounted to Present Value, as it already takes place in the present, as Year 0 represents the start of the project – effectively now.

Net present value

Once we have applied DCF to Blaise's forecasts it is a relatively simple step to use the **net present value** technique to assess viability. Add up all the discounted values, including the initial (negative) one. The sum of £1,978 is called the net present value (NPV), and all Blaise has to do to assess the project is to see whether it is positive or negative. If it were negative it would indicate that, on financial grounds at least, the project would lose her money. As it's positive – and a high figure of £1,978 at that – she can be in no doubt that, assuming her assumptions are correct, the project is a winner.

Fortunately, with modern-day spreadsheets, Blaise doesn't have to tinker with complicated formulas and mathematics to get her answer. All she needs to do is enter her forecasts onto the computer and then, in the cell where she wants the NPV to appear:

=NPV (interest rate, range of future values) + initial cost

In this case: =NPV(8%,cell range of first to last 3,000) + (−10,000)
If done correctly the answer £1,978 will appear.

Internal rate of return (IRR)

To make sense of NPV we have to express our result as an absolute amount (in Blaise's case £1,978) with accompanying interest rate (8%). For some non-financial people this is more than they can absorb without a quick lesson in the intricacies of investment appraisal.

Perhaps a simpler way of using DCF to help Blaise in her decision-making is to express the result as a percentage rather than as a monetary figure. IRR does exactly this by calculating the interest rate at which the NPV is zero. In this way the **internal rate of return** (IRR) of the project and the cost of capital cancel each other out to give neither surplus nor deficit.

Again, spreadsheets have made life easier in this respect and by entering:

=IRR(range of cells from initial cost to final future value)

The result in Blaise's case is 15%, so if she is borrowing funds at 8%, buying the machine will add value to her business.

Qualitative factors

As with all aspects in this book, money isn't everything. Of course, value for money is something we strive for most of the time, but we probably make a few decisions in life in which cost-effectiveness may not be our ultimate criterion for selection. Occasionally we may splash out and treat ourselves, regardless of the cost. Or we may take the opposite track and forego our own interests for reasons of fairness to others, family, charity or sustainability. In business, there may be many situations in which the NPV or IRR result may not be in the main yardstick for making a final decision. Perhaps the main lesson of this book is that, while the financial decision is usually present in our thinking, whether we are a student, employee, manager, owner or billionaire magnate, there may be other non-financial values which should be taken into account, such as environmental factors, corporate governance or corporate social responsibility.

Summary

This chapter has covered:

- The use of appropriate techniques to assess the financial viability of long-term projects.
- Simple, non–DCF methods of appraisal: payback and accounting rate of return (ARR).

- The principle of discounted cash flow to show the time value of money.
- DCF methods of appraisal: net present value (NPV) and internal rate of return (IRR).
- The importance of non-financial aspects in decision making.

Discussion Point 1: What elements should you include in a proposal for expenditure on an item of equipment you feel to be necessary?

Discussion Point 2: If someone presented such a proposal to you, what criteria would you use to assess it?

Discussion Point 3: How useful are formal investment appraisal techniques?

Exercise: City Rovers Football Club made a loss of £4 million last year, based on gate receipts totalling £28 million for the year. The club is considering the purchase of one of two professional players to resurrect its fortunes.

Geoff Ritchie is 20 years old and is considered to be a future star. His present club is asking for a transfer fee of £20 million (payable immediately), and he is prepared to sign a 5-year contract with Rovers for £80,000 a week. With Ritchie in the team, Rovers expect gate receipts to rise by at least 20%, and extra money from television, sponsorships, league placing, cup runs etc., of £18 million a year, and these figures to remain constant for the length of his contract. The club could expect at least £10 million from his transfer after 5 years.

Tom Bradford is 34 years old and an established international footballer who is prepared to sign for Rovers on a 2-year contract, after which he will retire. He would expect a salary of £30,000 a week and could be secured for a transfer fee of £1 million from his present club (payable immediately). His popularity would boost the gate by at least 40%, and he should attract an extra £6 million from television, etc.

The rate of interest applicable to the transaction is 12%, and the following is an extract from the present value table for £1:

	12%
Year 1	0.893
Year 2	0.797
Year 3	0.712
Year 4	0.636
Year 5	0.507

Assume that all costs are paid and revenues received at the end of each year.

Required

> Evaluate the financial results of enlisting each player by the net present value method, providing City Rovers with information to assist it in deciding which alternative to adopt.

14 What next?

The intention of this book is to give you a comprehensive overview of accounting in as succinct and painless a manner as possible, while still containing sufficient practice and detail to allow you to apply the concepts addressed, whether as a student or as a business practitioner. While dealing with both financial and management accounting, the main emphasis is on the future cost-control, income generation and managerial decision-making benefits which arise from the perceptive application of management accounting.

It is hoped that by reading *Management Accounting for Beginners* you will now have an understanding of the following:

Double-Entry Book-Keeping – a brief introduction to the function of keeping formal accounting records provides knowledge of the principles of double-entry debit and credit entry and the four main accounting books or ledgers and the significance, purpose and limitations of the trial balance.

Interpreting Financial Statements – identifying the key financial statements showing income generation, cash flow and financial position and demonstrating their composition and use and being able to analyse organisational performance in terms of profitability, liquidity, efficiency, gearing and investment.

Budgeting – as a fundamental exercise for most managers, budgeting is an important element of managerial control, giving you an awareness of the contribution that budgeting systems and processes lead to economic efficiency.

Cost Behaviour and Classification – knowledge of one of the most important tasks of management, controlling and reducing expenses, is vital in business. The principles of how costs behave and the relationship of costs to levels of operational activity should now be clear, as well as the categories used for identifying different types of cost.

Break-Even Analysis – managers can use cost volume profit analysis as a means of focusing on practical business needs and objectives and as an analytical tool for decision making and problem solving. The main business applications of the break-even concept can now be identified, explaining key terms and considering some of its problems and shortcomings.

Marginal and Absorption Costing – compares managerial and accounting approaches to corporate profitability issues and assesses the quantitative as well as qualitative factors to consider when faced with a choice of strategic options.

Overhead Recovery – when organisations cost their products or services they must be acutely aware of the hidden, indirect costs which must be recouped, as well as the more visible costs of materials and labour. The traditional methods of calculating costs in order to arrive at a fair and viable market price are explained.

Activity-Based Costing – fixed costs dominate the cost structures of most organisations nowadays. As managers are increasingly required to use every possible means to reduce corporate expenses, this dominance calls for analysis and explanation. The use of activity-based costing (ABC), an approach initiated in the 1980s, is explained as a reliable and representative basis for tracking and controlling costs.

Performance Measurement – as so many organisations use key performance indicators to gauge how well (or badly) employees and departments function, constructive ways of assessing achievement are discussed. The balanced scorecard provides a useful foundation, using core strategy and senior management support in order to devise meaningful measures of performance.

Variance Analysis – this technique observes and analyses the difference between projected figures within budgets and actual results. It serves as a sound and valuable business discipline, providing the basis of an effective system of management control. Standard costing, the method shown here, is widely used and can be very valuable in turnaround situations.

Responsibility Accounting – corporate decentralisation has major implications for costing. Allocating costs to products across an organisation is now widely regarded as incompatible with good cost control because it cannot accurately identify areas of responsibility. The system known as responsibility accounting, in which costs and revenues are traced to the people or departments that have incurred them, is examined here.

Investment Appraisal – formal methods for evaluating the success of long-term projects are presented in this chapter. Anything from buying a mobile phone for a few pounds to accomplishing a multi-million-pound corporate takeover can serve as a vehicle for the application of a number of techniques designed to assess the financial merits of whether to go ahead with a project.

For further reading, to explore the subject of accounting in greater detail, you can refer to:

Financial Accounting: A Concepts-Based Introduction by David Kolitz (2016). This Routledge textbook helps students understand the concepts that underpin the application of accounting theory to help solve accounting problems and includes extracts from financial statements, definitions of key terms and exam examples, along with real-life examples to support class work.

Another recommendation is *Financial Accounting* by Bev Vickerstaff and Parminder Johal (2013). Students looking for a focused introduction to financial accounting will appreciate this book, published by Routledge, which provides accessible yet stimulating introductions to core business studies modules. The text comes with additional support materials including interactive multiple choice questions.

For more of a management accounting focus there is *Management Accounting in a Dynamic Environment* by Cheryl S. McWatters and Jerold L. Zimmerman (2016), again published by Routledge. With international examples that bring the current business environment to the forefront, problems and cases to promote critical thinking, and online support for students and instructors, this book provides students and managers with an understanding and appreciation of the strengths and limitations of an organization's accounting system and enables them to be intelligent and critical users of the system.

Good luck in your pursuit of accounting knowledge!

15 Solutions to exercises

Chapter 2: Double-Entry Book-Keeping

Clarence Park's Trial Balance as at 31 December	Dr (£)	Cr (£)
Cash	5,850	
Bank	10,300	
Equity		15,000
Accounts payable		2,900
Accounts receivable	400	
Discounts allowed	60	
Discounts received		100
Purchases	3,500	
Purchase returns		100
Sales		4,600
Sales returns	200	
Bank loan		5,000
Interest	400	
Rent	200	
Drawings	300	
Carriage inwards	100	
Wages	1,000	
Bad debts	190	
Sundry expenses	100	
Disposal of machine (loss)	100	
Vehicle	5,000	
	27,700	27,700

Chapter 3: Interpreting Financial Statements

Harry Stoke *Income Statement for the day*	£	£
Sales		700
Purchases	2,000	
Less Closing stock	1,500	
Cost of sales		500
Gross Profit		200
Less Rent	500	
Petrol	50	
Loss		550
		(350)

Statement of Financial Position as at the end of the day				
Non-current Assets			Equity	
Van		8,000		
			Loss	(350)
Current Assets			Non-current Liabilities	
Inventories	1,500			20,000
Accounts receivable	700			
Cash	11,450		Current Liabilities	
		3,650	Accounts payable	2,000
		21,650		21,650

Chapter 4: Budgeting

Stapleton Services plc (in £000)

Forecast Income Statement for year ending ...

Revenue (100,000 hours × £200)		20,000
Direct costs (100,000 hours × £40)	4,000	
Administration	5,000	
Commissions (10% of £20m)	2,000	
Loan Interest (Bank 10% of £4m)	400	
(Debenture 5% of £2m)	100	
Bad Debts (25% of £2m)	500	
General Expenses	6,000	
		18,000
Profit Before Tax		2,000
Corporation Tax (20%)		400
Profit After Tax		1,600
Dividends (8p × 10m shares)		800
Retained Profits (added to reserves)		800

Forecast Balance Sheet as at ....

Non-current Assets	*Cost*	*Dep*	*Net*
Land and Buildings	12,000	2,600	9,400
Office furniture	3,000	1,300	1,700
Motor vehicles	6,000	4,100	1,900
(500 nbv-100 dep-200 sold+500 bought)	21,000	8,000	13,000

Current Assets		
Inventories		500
Accs rec'ble (36.5/365 days × £20m)		2,000
Cash and bank (missing figure)		4,900
		7,400

Current Liabilities		
Accs payable ((£500k/125) × 100)	400	
Corporation Tax	400	
Dividend proposed	800	
		1,600

Net current assets		5,800
		18,800
Equity		
10m Ordinary Shares	8,000	
Reserves	4,800	
		12,800
Long Term Liabilities		
Bank loans at 10%	4,000	
Debentures at 8%	2,000	
		6,000
		18,800

Cash Budget for year ending ...

Opening cash balance		4,000

RECEIPTS

Cash from fees (2m–0.5m+20m–2m)		19,500
(i.e. last year Debtors–Bad Debts+Rev–this year Debtors)		23,500

PAYMENTS

Tax and Div paid (1m + 1m)	2,000	
Cash expenses (18m–0.5m bd–1m dep)	16,500	
Creditors paid (0.5m–0.4m)	100	
		18,600
Closing cash balance		4,900

Chapter 5: Cost Behaviour and Classification

a)

	Hippodrome	Royal	Net cost/benefit of Hippodrome
Seats	5,000	3,000	
Charge (£)	20	25	
	£	£	£
Revenue	100,000	75,000	25,000
(seats × entry charge)			
Costs			
Cost of hire	(1,000)	(1,000)	0
Insurance	(2,000)	-	(2,000)
Depreciation	(1,000)	(1,000)	0
Administration	(6,000)	(6,000)	0
Extra travel	(12,750)	-	(12,750)
Lost fund raising	(800)	-	(800)
Printing	(8,000)	(8,000)	0
Programme	2 (10,000)	(6,000)	(4,000)
Publicity	(1,800)	(1,800)	0
Profit	56,650	51,200	5,450

b) Explanation should outline the 3 relevant cost criteria: future, cash flows and differential costs. Mention should be made of fixed/variable costs, sunk costs, opportunity cost, etc.

Chapter 6: Break-even Analysis

Speedwell

Units	FC (£)	VC (£)	TC (£)	TR (£)	P/L
0	3,000	0	3,000	0	(3,000)
50	3,000	3250	6,250	3,750	(2,500)
100	3,000	6500	9,500	7,500	(2,000)
150	3,000	9750	12,750	11,250	(1,500)
200	3,000	13000	16,000	15,000	(1,000)
250	3,000	16250	19,250	18,750	(500)
300	3,000	19500	22,500	22,500	0
350	3,000	22750	25,750	26,250	500
400	3,000	26000	29,000	30,000	1,000

Break-even Formula = FC divided by contribution or 3,000/(75–65)
                                = 300 units

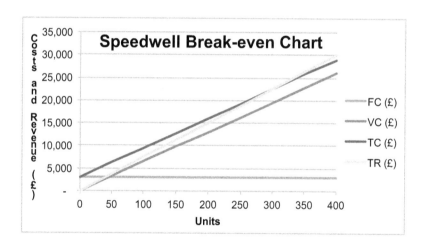

Chapter 7: Marginal and Absorption Costing

Fishponds Ltd

Income Statement for the coming year (as normal)	£	£
Revenue (10,000 units at £250)		2,500,000
Costs:		
Materials	800,000	
Labour	900,000	
Variable production overhead	100,000	
Fixed production overhead	300,000	
Administration expenses	120,000	
Rent	80,000	
		2,300,000
Profit		200,000
Fishponds' cost breakdown: Total Variable Costs		1,800,000
Total Fixed Costs		500,000

Option A:

Variable, or Marginal, cost per unit (£1,800,000 ÷ 10,000 units)	£180
Contribution per unit (£190–£180)	£10
Total contribution (1,000 units × £10)	£10,000

Accepting Option A will increase profits by £10,000

Option B

Variable, or Marginal, cost per unit (£1,800,000 ÷ 10,000 units)	£180
Extra machine costs per annum (£10,000 depreciation + £11,000 running costs)	£21,000
Machine costs expressed on a per unit basis (£21,000 ÷ 1,000 units)	£21
Contribution per unit (£200 – £201)	−1
Total contribution (1,000 units × − £1)	−1,000

Accepting Option B will incur losses of £1,000

So A adds £10,000 to profit, while B reduces profits by £1,000. However, always consider that there might be non-financial or qualitative aspects such as new markets, prestige, foreign advantages, new machine, environment, etc. which may make B a viable option.

Chapter 8: Overhead Recovery

SOLUTION: Rangeworthy	(in £)		
1 (a) and (b) **(i) Labour hour rate**	*Manufacturing*	*Assembly*	*Total*
Supervisors' wage (actual)	1,000	1,000	2,000
Indirect labour (actual)	2,000	1,000	3,000
Rent and rates (assessed on basis of floor area ie 2:1)	6,000	3,000	9,000
Total	9,000	5,000	14,000
	£9,000	£5,000	
	10,000 lab hrs =90p per lab/hr	25,000 lab hrs =20p per lab/hr	
(ii) Machine hour rate			
Power (assessed on basis of machine hrs ie 2:3)	1,200	1,800	3,000
Repairs (actual)	1,500	1,100	2,600
Depreciation (on basis of plant value ie 5:4)	500	400	900
	3,200	3,300	6,500
	£3,200	£3,300	
	2,000 mach hrs =£1.60per m/hr	3,000 mach hrs =£1.10 per m/hr	

2. Using the above rates, the overhead apportionment for the Whitehall is therefore:

	(in £)		
	Manufacturing	*Assembly*	
Labour (1,000 hrs × 90p)	900	100	(500 hrs × 20p)
Machine (400 hrs × £1.60)	640	660	(600 hrs × £1.1)
Total overheads	1540	760	

The overall cost for Whitehalls is:

Materials	200	100
Labour	300	600
Overhead	1540	760
	2040	1460

So each Whitehall costs (£2,040 + £1,460) = £3,500

Chapter 9: Activity Based Costing

SOLUTION: Hotwells

1. Overhead absorption rate is currently based on the specialist hours worked, which are:

X: (£80/£20) x 1,000 clients = 4,000 hrs   Y: (£100/£20) x 2,000 clients = 10,000 hrs
<u>Overheads = £700,000</u> = £50 specialist labour hours 14,000 hrs
Therefore X's overhead is 4 hrs x £50 = £200 and Y's is 5 hrs x £50 = £250

2.	*X*	*Y*	*Total*
Services provided	1,000	2,000	
	£k	£k	£k
Fees	<u>350</u>	<u>800</u>	<u>1150</u>
Specialist labour	80	200	280
Overheads	<u>200</u>	<u>500</u>	<u>700</u>
Profit	70	100	170

3.	*X*	*Y*	*Total*
	£k	£k	£k
Admin (based on staffing)	120	80	200
Promotion/liaison (Basd on staffing)	180	20	200
Buildings (based on usage)	<u>210</u>	<u>90</u>	<u>300</u>
Total	510	190	700

So the ABC for each provision of X is £510,000/1,000 clients = £510 and for Y it is £190,000/2,000 clients = £95

4.	*X*	*Y*	*Total*
Services provided	1,000	2,000	
	£k	£k	£k
Fees	350	800	1150
Specialist labour	80	200	280
Overheads	510	190	700
Profit/(Loss)	(240)	410	170

5. The prices should be based on the following cost of service (with the ABC derived from part 3 above):

	X	*Y*
	£k	£k
Fees	<u>350</u>	<u>400</u>
Specialist labour	80	100
ABC overheads	<u>510</u>	<u>95</u>
Cost of service	<u>590</u>	<u>195</u>
Profit/(Loss)	(240)	205

The price of X in particular should be re-examined. As ever, non-financial factors must be considered as well.

Clifton KPIs

	This Year	_Last Year_
Number of clients	430	395
Consultants	70	63
Admin/support staff	57	50
Training expenditure (£)	100,670	99,670
Revenue from fees (£)	5,590,879	4,890,804

Financial				_% Change_
An alternative financial measure to revenue per client is:				
Av. revenue per consultant (£)	_[fees/consultants]_	79,870	77,632	2.88%

Customer				
An alternative customer measure to clients per consultants is:				
Clients per admin member	_[clients/admin]_	7.54	7.90	(4.51%)

Internal				
An alternative internal measure to support staff per consultant is:				
Av. Revenue per employee (£)	_[admin/consultants]_ _[fees/cons+admin]_	44,023	43,281	1.71%

Innovation & Learning				
An alternative I and L measure to training per staff member is:				
Training exp. as % of turnover	_[exp/fees]_	1.80%	2.04%	(11.64%)

There are other possibilities so well done if you have thought of other valid performance measures.

Chapter 11: Variance Analysis

SOLUTION: Ashton District Council

First of all the budget must be adjusted to the actual level of activity (18,000 miles) rather than the 20,000 originally planned. The expected usage of materials for only 18,000 miles would be 900 kg (the standard usage works out at 0.05 kg per mile), labour would be 4,500 hours (at a quarter of an hour per mile), and fixed overhead (at the £7 direct labour hour rate) would be £31,500.

Adjusted budget for year:

	£	£
Income: 18,000 miles of cleaning at £6 per mile		108,000
Direct materials: 900 kg at £7 per kilo	6,300	
Direct labour: 4,500 hours at £5.00 per hour	22,500	
Fixed overheads: 4,500 hrs at £7	31,500	
		60,300
Adjusted Budgeted Profit		47,700

Variances

Income:

$$TMV = £108000 - £108000 = 0$$

$$IMPV = £0 \times 18000 \text{miles} = 0 \qquad IMVoV = 0\text{mls} \times £6 = 0$$

Materials:

$$TMV = £6300 - £7200 = £900A$$

$$MPV = £1 \times 1200\text{kg} = £1200F \qquad MUV = 300\text{kg} \times £7 = £2100A$$

Labour:

$$TLV = £22500 - £24750 = £2250A$$

$$LRV = 50\text{p} \times 4500\text{hrs} = £2250A \qquad LEV = 0\text{hrs} \times £5 = 0$$

Overheads:

$$TOV = £41000 - £31500 = £9500A$$

$$OExV = £41000 - £35000 = £6000A \qquad OVoV = £31500 - £35000 = £3500A$$

In each case check that the two subvariances sum to the overall variance. To reconcile the budgeted profit to the actual profit:

	£
Adjusted Budgeted profit		47,700
Income variance	0
Materials variance	900A
Labour variance	2,250A
Fixed o/h variance	9,500A
Total variance	12,650A
Actual profit	35,050

Chapter 12: Responsibility Accounting

Downend

a) Profitability statement for the year:

	£	£
Income (4,000 hours of service A @ £50)		200,000
(12,000 units of full service @ £90)		1,080,000
Costs (16,000 hrs of A @ £30)	480,000	
(12,000 hrs of B @ £25)	300,000	
Fixed Costs	400,000	
		1,180,000
Profit		100,000

Another way of looking at this is the contribution approach, which focuses on the contribution made by each service: 4,000 (A) x £20 plus 12,000 (A and B) x £35 equals £500,000 minus the fixed costs of £400,000 to give profits of £100,000. You should be capable of using both methods.

b) Profitability statement showing separate departmental profits:

	Dept A £	Dept B £	Total £
Income (4,000 @ £50)	200,000		
(12,000 @ £45)	540,000		
	740,000		
(12,000 @ £90)		1,080,000	1,820,000
(12,000 @ £45)		540,000	1,020,000
Costs (16,000 @ £30)	480,000		
(12,000 @ £25)		300,000	300,000
Fixed Costs	200,000	200,000	400,000

Profit	680,000	1,040,000	1,720,000
	60,000	40,000	100,000

Looking at the two departments, can you see what two financial factors have determined how the profits have been split? The answer is (i) the *transfer price* and (ii) the sharing of the *fixed costs*. If these two figures were renegotiated, they would result in the same £100,000 overall profit being redistributed between A and B. The fact that A earns more than B above has nothing do with that department's ability or efficiency, yet sometimes responsibility accounting has been used to make judgements of that kind.

c) The main feature of this new situation is that B will have to increase profitability by a total of £60,000 (savings of £5 on 12,000 units of the full service), but A will be severely hit as its own sales of 12,000 hours to B will collapse. Overall, Downend will suffer, with the best case being a loss of £20,000 (A will make losses of £120,000 against B's profit of £100,000), but that assumes that A's outside sales are unaffected by the new entrant - an unlikely scenario given the competitor's supply for a similar service.

This example highlights the **three basic principles** which must be considered before tampering with a workable situation by introducing responsibility centres:

1) There should be goal *congruency* between divisions, and managers should not seek policies which are harmful to the rest of the organisation.
2) Each section should be *autonomous* with profits independent of other departments.
3) If divisions are to be assessed under responsibility accounting, such judgements should be a *reliable measure* of their performance, rather than of the financial aspects of the reorganisation (i.e. dependent on the transfer pricing and the allocation of fixed costs).

Chapter 13: Investment Appraisal

SOLUTION: City Rovers FC

	Ritchie	Bradford		
	£	£		
Transfer	20,000,000	1,000,000		
Wages per wk	80,000	30,000		
Rise in gate	20%	40%	Loss	4,000,000
			Receipts	28,000,000
			pa	
Gate pa	5,600,000	11,200,000		
TV money	18,000,000	6,000,000		
Wages pa	4,160,000	1,560,000		

Ritchie

	Out		In			
Year	wages	transfer	gate	transfer	TV, etc	NCF
0		(20,000,000)				(20,000,000)
1	(4,160,000)		5,600,000		18,000,000	19,440,000
2	(4,160,000)		5,600,000		18,000,000	19,440,000
3	(4,160,000)		5,600,000		18,000,000	19,440,000
4	(4,160,000)		5,600,000		18,000,000	19,440,000
5	(4,160,000)		5,600,000	10,000,000	18,000,000	29,440,000
					NPV	55,751,118

Bradford

Year	Out		In			NCF
	wages	*transfer*	*gate*	*transfer*	*TV, etc*	
0		(1,000,000)				(1,000,000)
1	(1,560,000)		11,200,000		6,000,000	15,640,000
2	(1,560,000)		11,200,000	0	6,000,000	15,640,000
					NPV	25,432,398

Ritchie's transfer will earn NPV of nearly £56m over 5 years.

However, Bradford's transfer will earn more than £25m in only 2 years.

Both options are attractive - depends on long- or short-term preference and risk and uncertainty considerations.

Index

Note: Page numbers with *f* indicate figures; those with *t* indicate tables.

For Product Safety Concerns and Information please contact our EU
representative GPSR@taylorandfrancis.com
Taylor & Francis Verlag GmbH, Kaufingerstraße 24, 80331 München, Germany

www.ingramcontent.com/pod-product-compliance
Ingram Content Group UK Ltd.
Pitfield, Milton Keynes, MK11 3LW, UK
UKHW020934180425
457613UK00019B/385